THE
NAVAJO
AND HIS
BLANKET

PISCHEL YEARBOOKS, INC.

P.O. Box 36, Marceline, Missouri 64658

PISCHEL YEARBOOKS, INC.

P.O. Box 36, Marceline, Missouri 64658

THE NAVAJO AND HIS BLANKET

BY

U. S. HOLLISTER

DENVER, COLO

The Rio Grande Press, Inc.

GLORIETA, NEW MEXICO · 87535

© 1972
The Rio Grande Press, Inc.,
Glorieta, N. M. 87535

First edition from which this edition was
reproduced was supplied by
FRED ROSENSTOCK, Books
1228 E. Colfax Ave.,
Denver, Colo. 80218

Library of Congress Cataloging in Publication Data

Hollister, Uriah S   1838-1929.
   The Navajo and his blanket.

   (A Rio Grande classic)
   Reprint of the 1903 ed.
   1. Navaho Indians--Industries. 2. Indians of
North America--Textile industry and fabrics.
I. Title.
E99.N3H7 1972   970.3   72-10567
ISBN 0-87380-097-4

A RIO GRANDE CLASSIC
First published in 1903

Second Printing 1974

The Rio Grande Press, Inc.
GLORIETA, NEW MEXICO · 87535

Publisher's Preface

Recently we went to Denver, and we never go to that lovely city without visiting our great and good friend Fred Rosenstock. We chatted quite awhile about the vagaries of the book business and the art business--Fred's book store on Colfax Avenue is more like an art gallery, these days, than a book store--finally getting around to books worth reprinting. We mentioned the continuing heavy demand we have for our books on Navajo weaving (Amsden's *Navajo Weaving;* Reichard's trilogy *Navajo Shepherd and Weaver, Spider Woman,* and *Dezba, Navajo Woman of the Desert,* and George Wharton James' *Indian Blankets and Their Makers),* we wondered if there were any other old titles worth a new edition.

Fred bounced up out of his chair, hurriedly ventured into his mysterious "collection" room upstairs and came back in a few moments triumphantly waving a practically mint first edition of this book. The author, Fred explained (as only he can), lived in Denver when he wrote and privately published this beautiful title (1903). We couldn't afford to pay Fred's price ($150.00) for the rare item, but since in our reprinting we do no harm to a first edition, he was quite willing to lend it to us. We were eager to borrow, so here, now, you hold in your hands another beautiful Rio Grande Classic.

While this book was first published in 1903, it was apparently "in preparation" for several years before that--perhaps as early as 1890. Author Uriah S. Hollister, according to his obituary, was a man of considerable social, economic and political stature; he was totally a man of his milieu. The terms he sometimes used to refer to male and female American Indians may sound offensive today to the hypersensitive, superbleeders for "minority" ethnic groups, but unfortunately, that's the way history is; that is certainly the way it was at the turn of the century. For those who do not know any better, the word "squaw" is an Indian term, and not a term of derogation. The term "buck" to describe an Indian man came into the American lexicon as early as the 17th century and continued in current usage until as late as the end of World War I. No doubt it was used pejoratively by some, but by others it was simply a word that denoted a male Indian and held no subtle nuance.

History is being re-written today on all sides, just as in Orwell's grim fantasy *1984,* to conform to the way the modern "sociologist" thinks history should have been (if you do not believe this, try reading most contemporary high school world and American history textbooks). That such rewriting is both deliberate distortion and outright deception makes no difference at all to the "historians" doing it, the total effect is to make some aspects of history something they never were. In any case, author Hollister's use of certain terms that are not in use today was widely and completely acceptable lexicon in his day and age; perhaps today's terms may seen as abominable in 2041 A.D. as yesterday's terms are today.

We called on our friend Alys Freeze, head of the Western History Collection of the Denver Public Library, for information about Uriah Hollister. Presently she sent us a stat of a microfilm obituary that appeared in The Rocky Mountain News of September 9, 1929. We would liked to have reproduced the obituary facsimile, as we have done in other of our titles, but the copy came as a photostat from a microfilm and while legible, was not reproducible. We copy herewith:

> "Funeral services for Uriah S. Hollister, former prominent Denver oil man and G.A.R. veteran, will be held in Hollywood Calif., this week.
>
> "Mr. Hollister died at Hollywood Monday, within less than a month of his 91st birthday, his son, James M. Hollister, 450 S. Marion St., was informed.
>
> "From 1894 until his retirement in 1912, Mr. Hollister was a leading figure in business and social circles of Denver. He was sent here by the Standard Oil Co. interests to help build up the Continental Oil Co. He was vice president of that company when he retired.
>
> "When the Civil War started, Mr. Hollister enlisted in a company of Wisconsin volunteers. He served during the entire conflict and was discharged with the rank of captain.
>
> "Shortly after the war Mr. Hollister began his career in the oil business by becoming manager of an agency for the Standard Oil Co. at Marquette, Mich.
>
> "Mr. Hollister had a hobby of collecting unusual articles of American Indian and Chinese craftsmanship. His collection was regarded as one of the finest in the country. He also was author of a book on Navajo rugs, which was considered an outstanding text on the subject. As plates for this book were destroyed by fire, copies of it are very rare, relatives said.
>
> "Two years after his retirement, Mr. Hollister and his wife went to California, where they had lived ever since.
>
> "Mr. Hollister was born at Dryden, N.Y., Sept. 11, 1838. He was a graduate of Williams College.
>
> "Besides his son here, he is survived by his wife, two daughters, Mrs. Roy Willard and Mrs. J.G.T. Moore, both of Hollywood; another son, Leonard Hollister, Sebago Lake, Maine; a brother,

Warren C. Hollister, Los Angeles, and a sister, Mrs. A.H. Kendrick, Delevan, Wis."

Technically, we have changed the appearance of the book from that of the first edition. The original edition is rather oddly sized, being seven and one-half inches horizontally and nine and one-half inches vertically. We have enlarged the pages in reproduction to eight and one half by eleven inches. This makes the book not only easier to read and handle, but enlarges considerably the artwork and color plates. Those who know the first edition will note that we have incorporated into the cover design an enlarged replica of the original title design. We thought it attractive and well done, so we used it again.

We have also, for technical reasons, repositioned the ten color plates; the plates are referred to in the text only by plate number, not by position. Hence, we corrected the "List of Illustrations" to show the correct new position of the color plate.

This is the 91st title we have published, and the 89th beautiful Rio Grande Classic; the other two titles we call Rio Grande Press Pictorial Specials.

Robert B. McCoy

La Casa Escuela
Glorieta, N.M. 87535
December 1972

"HOMEWARD BOUND"

THE NAVAJO AND HIS BLANKET

BY

U. S. HOLLISTER

DENVER, COLO.

THE PRINTING AND THREE-COLOR WORK BY
THE UNITED STATES COLORTYPE CO.
AND
HALF-TONE WORK BY
THE WILLIAMSON-HAFFNER ENGRAVING CO.
DENVER, COLORADO

CONTENTS

INTRODUCTION 9

"THE NORTH AMERICAN INDIAN" (*Sprague*). . . . 13

THE RED MAN 17

A SUMMER DAY IN NAVAJO LAND 21

THE NAVAJO LAND 27

THE NAVAJO 41

HABITATIONS 65

THE BEGINNING 77

ANOTHER STEP 83

THE BLANKET 91

CONCLUSION 129

LIST OF ILLUSTRATIONS

COLORED PLATES

FACING PAGE

PLATE I — One-half of a Navajo "Squaw-dress" of the period between 1840 and 1860 - - - - - - - - - - - - - 10

PLATE II — An old example of Navajo work in pink bayeta, native dyes, made about 1850 - - - - - - - - - - - - 26

PLATE III — An old blanket of native wool in natural colors and native dyes 42

PLATE IV — A curious and rare old blanket of sacred significance, woven about 1845 - - - - - - - - - - - - - - 56

PLATE V — A modern rug-blanket, made in 1891 - - - - - - 72

PLATE VI — An old specimen bearing the Head Chief's emblem, of the period of 1865 - - - - - - - - - - - - - 89

PLATE VII — A valuable old bayeta blanket made about 1840 - - - - 106

PLATE VIII — A combination of bayeta and Germantown yarn - - - - 122

PLATE IX — A Navajo beauty, wholly of Germantown yarn, about twenty-five years old - - - - - - - - - - - - - 123

PLATE X — Another fine example of Navajo weaving, entirely of Germantown yarn - - - - - - - - - - - - - 138

ENGRAVINGS

"Homeward Bound" - - - - Frontispiece

Portrait of the Author - - - - - - 9

Group of Navajos Visiting Santa Fe - - 16

LIST OF ILLUSTRATIONS— *Continued*

PAGE

FIGURE 1—* * "in most characteristics entirely different from the aborigines of any other country" - - - - - 17

FIGURE 2—* * "where two mountains look at each other across a canon" - - - - - - - - 21

FIGURE 3—A Navajo Summer Hogan - - - - - - 24

FIGURE 4—* * "a mountain, mesa and valley country" - - 27

FIGURE 5—A Cliff Dweller's Sandal; upper and lower sides - - 31

FIGURE 6—A Navajo "Sweat House" - - - - - - 38

FIGURE 7—* * "he struts and poses in great style until he scents his mother-in-law" - - - - - - 41

FIGURE 8—Navajos Worshiping the Elements - - - - 46

FIGURE 9—Navajo Indians Trading - - - - - 51

FIGURE 10—A Navajo Silversmith - - - - - - 58

FIGURE 11—* * "may be almost anything that can be considered a shelter" - - - - - - - - - 65

FIGURE 12—A Navajo Winter Hogan - - - - - 68

FIGURE 13—A More Elaborate Winter Hogan - - - - 74

FIGURE 14—* * "familiar landmarks today, but which were far more populous then than now" - - - - - - 77

FIGURE 15—"At San Ildelfonso * * he built the first church in New Mexico" - - - - - - - - - 83

FIGURE 16—* * "there was then, as now, a Navajo flock in every valley" - - - - - - - - - 91

FIGURE 17—A Navajo Woman Carding Wool - - - - 100

FIGURE 18—A Navajo Woman Spinning Wool - - - - 110

FIGURE 19—A Navajo Weaver - - - - - - - 120

FIGURE 20—* * "the young Navajo woman in her bridal array" - 129

FIGURE 21—A View in Zuni - - - - - - - 134

FIGURE 22—Navajos Gazing Upon A Railroad Train - - - 142

INTRODUCTION

WITH the passing of the North American Indians from their native condition there is an increasing interest in all that relates to them, to their origin, and to their modes of life before they were disturbed by the influences of advancing civilization. In the sequence of events it will not be long until they will live only in history; and therefore, realizing that this fate awaits them in the near future, we are collecting and recording all information we can obtain concerning their legends, traditions, beliefs, habits, manners, customs, and handiwork, and are eager to witness their tribal ceremonies and religious rites before the encroachments of the white man bring about their discontinuance. Every fact pertaining to their lives that we gather and record, and every article of their production that we obtain and preserve, will be of value to coming generations, and add to the stock of material available to future historians of this remarkable race of men.

Our researches along these lines bring us into contact with the structures and other remains of those strange and unknown peoples, the Cliff Dwellers and the Mound Builders, who were certainly far antecedent to our Indians in their occupation of our country. We study with intense interest their surviving monuments and other evidences of their presence here in the remote past in our still baffled efforts to determine who and what they were and how and when they lived; and treasure their lesser relics—their implements, pottery, and woven fabrics—as mementos of vanished races who, as we have many reasons for believing, may have risen and flourished long before the Christian era.

In decorating our homes with fine examples of our Indians' barbaric work which we willingly purchase at almost any price, we gratify our love for curious things and yield to our fancy for unusual embellishments; but in doing so we may also be building better than we know. Collections of the implements of domestic use, and of warfare, and of the clothing and ornaments, made by the Indians of our eastern coast in the time when our Pilgrim Fathers landed, would be of great value now; and collections assembled by us of similar articles made by the Indians of the present day will be hereafter of great ethnological and historic value.

As Indian wars have gone out of fashion, present-time products of Indian handiwork, among which general attention is divided, are basketry, beadwork, buckskin garments, necklaces, pottery, and the Navajo blanket. The more conspicuous of these, and toward which the greatest interest is directed, are the basket and the blanket. Basket-making covers a wide range of territory, the art being practiced by many tribes, who produce an almost endless variety of forms and patterns. From Alaska southward along our western coast and in the Rocky Mountain region, wherever there is an Indian tribe or clan, we may find the native-made basket in some form either for utilitarian, ceremonial, or ornamental purposes.

Among primitive people everywhere in the world the basket was the parent of textile fabrics; the art of weaving baskets having preceded that of weaving cloth, and having suggested the latter, among all races. How little we appreciate these early efforts of aboriginal men who gathered bark and twigs, or fibrous leaves of

Plate I—One-half of a Navajo "Squaw-dress," of the period
between 1840 and 1860.

plants, and formed them into rude receptacles for domestic use, and later developed the rudimentary art into one producing rough coverings for their bodies! In the fact that the oldest-known pieces of pottery bear marks of having been formed inside a basket, we have evidence that basketry preceded pottery; the basket-covering having been burned away, thus removing the mold and baking the pottery at the same time. It is difficult to realize that all the luxurious, beautiful, and useful fabrics produced by our modern looms had their origin in the exceedingly crude basket-weaving done by people living in a state of barbarism, if not of savagery. Collecting and studying Indian baskets possess much fascination for all who do so, and will long be in high favor among lovers of barbaric art.

But the Navajo blankets are peculiarly attractive to those who become familiar with their remarkable qualities and very interesting history. Indeed they are unique among Indian products, and may be said to stand aloof from all the others. Made by only one tribe, they have characteristics that no other people try to imitate; and at this time are attracting probably more attention than any other articles of Indian manufacture.

My interest in these really wonderful products of the simple looms of the Navajos dates from the first year of my residence in the Rocky Mountain country, and has remained unabated through the twenty years or more that have elapsed since. During this period I have had many opportunities to learn something about the aboriginal people of Colorado, Utah, New Mexico, and Arizona, having frequently visited the wigwams and wickyups of the Utes and of the Apaches, the adobe villages of the Pueblos, and the hogans of the Navajos. Though my boyhood years were spent on the pioneer line, and among my earlier recollections are those of Chippewa Indians calling in bands at my father's house in southern Wisconsin when that part of the country was practically a wilderness, I have never been in sympathy with those who think "the only good Indians are dead ones." There are many good Indians, and also many bad ones. But it might be worth while to remember that not all white men are good.

For some material used in the preparation of this little volume I am indebted to Pike's "Account" of his famous expedition, Major Emory's "Notes of a Military Reconnoissance," Governor Prince's "Story of New Mexico," and to the Reports of the Smithsonian Institution's Bureau of Ethnology; but its contents represent to a greater extent the results of my own observations and researches supplemented by information received from many good friends in the Navajo land.

The colored plates are direct reproductions from blankets in my collection, while the title page is by that conscientious painter of Indian life, Frank P. Sauerwen, three of whose pictures appear among the engravings. The other engravings are from photographs by P. E. Harroun, Sumner W. Matteson, Charles H. Goodman, Professor George H. Pepper of the Hyde expedition under the auspices of the American Museum of Natural History (New York), and by myself.

During the years in which I have been interested in the work of the Navajos and in collecting choice examples of their weaving, many questions concerning these people and their woven fabrics have been asked me; and it was in consequence of these frequent inquiries that I was prompted to prepare this little book. While it is far from a complete presentation of the subjects with which it deals, it may prove of value and interest to those who admire and buy Navajo blankets; and to them it is respectfully dedicated.

U. S. Hollister.

Denver, Colo., May, 1903.

THE NORTH AMERICAN INDIAN

(SPRAGUE.)

"Not many generations ago, where you now sit, encircled with all that exalts and embellishes civilized life, the rank thistle nodded in the wind, and the wild fox dug his hole unscared. Here lived and loved another race of beings. Beneath the same sun that rolls over your head, the Indian hunter pursued the panting deer; gazing on the same moon that smiles for you, the Indian lover wooed his dusky mate.

"Here, the wigwam-blaze beamed on the tender and helpless, and the council-fire glared on the wise and daring. Now, they dipped their noble limbs in your sedgy lakes, and now, they paddled the light canoe along your rocky shores. Here they warred; the echoing whoop, the bloody grapple, the defying death-song, all were here; and when the tiger-strife was over, here curled the smoke of peace.

"Here, too, they worshiped; and from many a dark bosom went up a fervent prayer to the Great Spirit. He had not written his laws for them on tables of stone, but he had traced them on the tables of their hearts. The poor child of Nature knew not the God of Revelation, but the God of the universe he acknowledged in everything around.

"He beheld him in the star that sank in beauty behind his lonely dwelling; in the sacred orb that flamed on him from his mid-day throne; in the flower that snapped in the morning's breeze; in the lofty pine that defied a thousand whirlwinds; in the timid warbler that never left its native grove; in the fearless eagle, whose untired pinion was wet in the clouds; in the worm that crawled at his feet; and in his own matchless form, glowing with a spark of that light, to whose mysterious source he bent in humble, though blind adoration.

"And all this has passed away. Across the ocean came a pilgrim bark, bearing the seeds of life and death. The former were sown for you; the latter sprung up in the path of the simple native. Two hundred years have changed the character of a great continent, and blotted forever from its face, a whole, peculiar people. Art has usurped the bowers of nature, and the anointed children of education have been too powerful for the tribes of the ignorant.

"Here and there, a stricken few remain, but how unlike their bold, untamed progenitors. The Indian of falcon glance and lion bearing, the theme of the touching ballad, the hero of the pathetic tale, is gone! and his degraded offspring crawls upon the soil, where he walked in majesty, to remind us how miserable is man, when the foot of the conqueror is on his neck.

"As a race, they have withered from the land. Their arrows are broken, their springs are dried up, their cabins are in the dust. The council-fire has long since gone out on the shore, and their war-cry is fast fading to the untrodden west. Slowly and sadly they climb the distant mountains, and read their doom in the setting sun. They are shrinking before the mighty tide which is pressing them away; they must soon hear the roar of the last wave, which will settle over them forever.

"Ages hence, the inquisitive white man, as he stands by some growing city, will ponder on the structure of their disturbed remains, and wonder to what manner of persons they belonged. They will live only in the songs and chronicles of their exterminators. Let these be faithful to their rude virtues, as men, and pay due tribute to their unhappy fate, as a people."

GROUP OF NAVAJOS VISITING SANTA FE
(From a photograph by P. E. Harroun)

THE RED MAN

FIGURE 1— * * "in most characteristics entirely different from the aborigines of any other country"

THE North American Indian has a strong personality; an individuality peculiar to himself. He is in most characteristics entirely different from the aborigines of any other country. Our Indian tribes may differ in details of habits, but they are remarkably alike in general. The men greatly dislike manual labor, or anything else that savors of drudgery. They are combative,—the warrior instinct being strong in all of them. To become a war-chief was the highest ambition of the young man: to be recognized as a great warrior, the highest ambition of the war-chief. Their war-songs took precedence over all the weird and uncanny vocal demonstrations that we call Indian song. To put on war-paint, and dress in the paraphernalia of war, was the highest gratification of their sense of barbaric pride. Their legends of battle, and of the victories won by their prowess, are among the more important of their stories; and they now tell us with great gusto of the brave deeds done by their people "long time ago."

Fond of the chase, our Indians are hunters of wild game almost by instinct. The "cunning of the fox" is met by the craft of the hunter, and to the weak trait in the habits of animal or bird appeal is made to the best advantage in effecting its capture. When possible, they seek timbered and well-watered regions as places of abode, and are cunning in woodcraft. The "four winds," or the four quarters of the compass, they know from the incline of the oak, or by the moss upon the rocks. They are not noted for ideal domestic virtues, and regard their women as of value only in proportion to the amount of manual labor they perform—to the extent that they lighten the burdens of their lords.

Indians are faithful friends, but implacable enemies; and are imitative of the white man chiefly in adopting his vices. While not disposed, as a general rule, to be truthful, they can be depended upon to lie to a white man who has lied to them. On the other hand, a white man who has dealt only in truth and fairness in his intercourse with them, may depend upon their integrity in all things. Therefore the white man's influence over them, is in proportion to the reputation he has established with them for regarding truth and honesty. It may be stated as a rule that if they are untruthful or dishonest themselves, they never fail to respect truth and honesty in others. They are in no sense emotional, and anything like sentiment is entirely foreign to their nature. Stoical to an exasperating degree, they will often persist in wearing a stolid, unchanged expression during one's efforts to amuse or abuse them. This is further illustrated by their temperate manifestations of either joy or sorrow, and the heroic fortitude with which they endure torture or other physical suffering.

All of them have some form of religion; its expression being the worship of natural phenomena. They worship the elements; the wind and the whirlwind; the gentle rain and the mountain storm; the storm clouds, the lightning and the thunder; the stars, the sun, and the moon. Birds and animals are also objects of adoration, but more often are regarded as means of communication with the elements, rather than as creatures to be directly worshiped. They bow in suppliant mood before idols of crude figures of stone or clay, or rude wood carvings. Their altars are often decorated with the feathers of birds, and with plumes of grass surmounting "sand paintings;" and surrounded by baskets of sacred meal and corn. Each uncouth figure represents the element with which they desire to communicate. They invoke these dumb gods, but beyond the mere figure, they see and invoke the element it represents.

For instance, the Pueblo Indian's God of Rain may be an ugly mass of sunburned clay, representing a human figure holding an olla, or water jar. While they pay tribute to it and ask that rain may fall upon their sun-scorched lands, they really look beyond the image, and fix their attention on the clouds from which they hope rain will come; and beyond the clouds to the governing Power of the universe.

The popular idea of the Indian's worship of idols is not entirely correct. He does not worship the idol, but that element in Nature represented by the idol. We venerate the cross, not because it has any power for good or evil, but because it is the emblem of the crucifixion. From a view-point of broad charity, we cannot deny the Indian's idol a place among the emblems of a world of worshipers. Who is competent to say that the Indian's worship of the grandeur of the firmament in which he sees and recognizes the power of an Omnipotent, is not as proper for him, as our worship is for us in any of the many ways enlightened people do so? The Indian has many idols: we have many forms. Read Prescott's "Conquest of Mexico," and then say by what human right the Spanish murderers of the peaceful Aztecs tore down their idols, and in their stead erected the cross literally stained with the blood of men who died defending their homes, and with the blood of helpless women and innocent children. If the broad mantle of charity be needed to cover the errors of the Spanish invader or those of his victims, let it be cast over the former.

While the Indian is not an ideal being, he is not lacking in many good qualities. Stolid, because he does not readily comprehend our ways, he really possesses a strong mentality, and understands natural phenomena better than we. He is not given to much talk, but that is not because of mental weakness. His memory is excellent, but he may often seem to forget, when it is not in his interest to remember. If he really does not understand, he is apt to attribute it to the supernatural. To him, everything in Nature partakes of the sacred; every element has a soul. The medicine man is his preacher, and his seer, or prophet; and is expected not only to cure disease, but to guard against it and against all other forms of evil; to ask favors of the supernatural, and to advise and direct in the forms of worship. Witchery is recognized, and considered a black art, and condemned to the extent of killing the witches, or of banishing them from the tribe. Some enlightened people possibly have set the example. We do not know whether the Indian believed in witchcraft before the landing of our good Pilgrim Fathers, or not. Let us not draw too close comparisons for fear of the result.

In conclusion, let us admit that the Indian is not a particularly lovable being. Possibly he will be when he learns to "love his neighbor as himself." For many generations he has considered the white man as his enemy. Why? Because he has hunted him from his native land; cheated and robbed him, and while a good white man was trying to convert him, a bad one was plying him with vile whisky. Sacred promises have been broken. He has been confined to barren reservations, forbidden to kill game, and hedged about by the white man's power; baffled by the white man's cunning—a cunning far deeper than his own. He has no way to turn but toward the setting sun; no voice to listen to but the voice of Fate, and that consigns him to the vale of extermination and says, "Good-bye!"

"Alas for them! their day is o'er,
Their fires are out from shore to shore."

A SUMMER DAY IN NAVAJO LAND

"An angel, robed in spotless white,
Bent down and kissed the sleeping night.
Night woke to blush: The sprite was gone.
Men saw the blush and called it Dawn."

FIGURE 2—* * "where two mountains look at each other across a canon"

SLOWLY the darkness of early morn falls back before the shafts of a rising sun. The keen arrows of light pierce its mantle, and it is driven fleeting to the west. The Sun is master: his morning rays dry the earth. The vapor rises from the streams in the valley, at first in little threads of white, like smoke from a dying camp fire; then gathering volume, it ascends until the course of the stream is plainly marked by a pearly white drapery that curtains the brightness of the new-born day. Lazily expanding, and growing darker, the mist assumes the form of threatening clouds, and these float up the canons and brush against the mountain sides, spraying the verdure with diamonds of dew, and baptizing it in the name of the glorious Orb of Day,—the Indians' "Father of All." Then they whiten again as they are bleached by the sun; and, stirred by the breeze, go tumbling over the mountains like great fleecy sheep at play. Beautiful in contrast with the purple haze of the ranges, the azure of the sky, and the light of the morning, yet they soon separate into slender strands of mist which wander off into space and are lost.

And now, everything is bathed in golden sunshine. The snow glistens on the peaks; the odor of pine and of cedar fills the air; the pure ozone tempts the lungs to full expansion. The world of wilderness is awake!

And this is Morning in Navajo land.

As the noontime approaches, the sun seems to pause overhead, where, in a dome of purest blue, it glows and burns, and parches the earth; but, under its influence, the valleys have revealed their wealth of wild flowers, cactus, sage and bright-leafed shrubs, that rival the barbaric colors of oriental drapery. The mountains with their gleaming caps of snow stand out in strong relief, in blue and gray and purple tints, and in ever-shifting lights and shadows. An eagle slowly and in great circles soars high in the blue sky. A coyote calls to his mate across the miles between mesa and mesa; or, in the shade of a cedar naps or idles the day away—a lazy vagabond, waiting for the night. On a distant trail, a Navajo on horseback, watching his sheep, shades his eyes and looks across the valley into the vast expanse of light; and in the distance he can see the smoke from the hut he calls home. He looks at the grandeur of the whole scene through the rarefied air of an elevation of more than a mile above the sea; through an atmosphere which, acting like the lens of a telescope, brings far-distant objects within easy range. The great panorama of mountain and plain, of mesa and valley, of arroya and canon, shaded here and there by pine and cedar, dwarfs every living thing. The stillness is the stillness of solitude; the beauty, the beauty of Nature undefiled.

And this is Mid-day in Navajo land.

As the afternoon grows old, the glare fades; and the sun, touching the rugged horizon, casts long shadows across the plains; and then, like a blazing meteor, drops out of sight behind the snow-capped mountains.

Now, turn your eyes to the west and look upon the glorious beauty of a sunset in this strange land. The peaks stand out like

FIGURE 3—A NAVAJO SUMMER HOGAN

sentinels guarding the retreat of day, and a blaze of light whitens the sunward side of those to the right and to the left. Fragments of gathering clouds, floating above in a sea of azure in which are blended tints of gray and green and yellow, are rich with the colors of red and gold and scarlet and purple which shift and change before our gaze as the misty masses drift with the evening breeze. Through this wealth of brilliant colors and mingled hues and tints the sun projects its rays in fan-like form far into space, the shafts and beams of light illuminating the whole, and completing a rare picture of magnificence that inspires feelings of reverence and humility in those who look upon it. You close your eyes, and wonder if anything else that is of this world can be so beautiful. The fiery glory behind the mountains dies down, but twilight lingers long as it slowly yields its beauty to the gathering shades of night.

And this is Evening in Navajo land.

One after another the stars appear; slowly and shyly at first, one here and one there; "then springing into myriads all at once." The rising moon is hidden by the mountains, and her soft white light, reflected on the clouds that float around and above the peaks, transforms them into masses of white and gold. As we stand in the deep shadow, the mountains are outlined in frosted silver by the light of the moon that we cannot see, and with this and the hues of the illuminated clouds before us, the grandly beautiful scene is like one we associate with the work of enchantment—a most wonderful combination of moonlight effects in the mountain regions of the Navajo land. As she rises, the moon's rim comes into view where two mountains look at each other across a canon (Figure 2); and, peering through this notch in the range, she seems to be asking: "Is it night? May I come?" But without awaiting our bidding she presents herself in all her splendor; and the mountains and cliffs and valleys—all the wide landscape around us, are flooded with her light and do homage to Her Majesty, the Queen of Night, —the Indians' "Mother of All Mankind."

The soughing of the pines as they are stirred by a rising breeze, is like the murmur of a distant sea, and warns us that the Storm King has had his battle array of thunder-clouds hidden behind the mountains. Now, as he leads them over the range, the wind rushes down the gorges, whirls around the foot-hills, and sweeps across the mesa and through the canons, raising great billows of dust. The air is "tremulous with the energy of an approaching storm." Suddenly, all is quiet; but soon the great rain-drops begin to fall—big warm tears of the clouds. Thicker and faster they come until the land is drenched, and new-made rivers roar in the canons, and flood the arroyas with their turbid waters. The clouds have swept over us, and in the silvery light that fills the night, we watch the retreating storm and hear the distant, sullen thunder, that rumbles like the cannonading of a retiring army that has spent its strength. Far-away dull flashes of lightning still tell of the storm that is gone; but the moon and the stars seem brighter than before, though low in the east is a touch of the faint first glow that heralds the coming of another morn.

And this was a summer day in Navajo land.

Plate II—An old example of Navajo work in "pink bayeta," native
wool and native dyes, made about 1850.

THE NAVAJO LAND

FIGURE 4—* * "a mountain, mesa and valley country"

A LAND of desert and of great brown plains; of rugged mountains and of sheltered valleys; of an azure sky, and a soft, winsome air that tempts one to rest and sleep; where the cold of winter is tempered by the warmth of a southern sun, and the summer heat is fanned to a delightful coolness by the ever-stirring breeze that comes down from snow-capped mountains, over the mesas and into the valleys, freighted with the breath of pines and cedars.

That portion of our sunny southwest occupied by the Navajo Indians, and set apart by the government as the Navajo Reservation, we shall call the Navajo land. Originally these people occupied a wide range of mountain and valley in southeastern Utah, southwestern Colorado, northwestern New Mexico and northeastern Arizona. Prior to 1846, they were bold marauders and, until tamed by American soldiers, were a menace to the pioneer line of civilization. In 1867 the present reservation, located in northwestern New Mexico, and northeastern Arizona, with a small area in southeastern Utah, was assigned them. While this reservation does not nearly cover the original area occupied by the Navajos prior to 1863, it is entirely within the lines of their first occupation. The reservation contains 12,000 square miles, or 7,680,000 acres, equal to the combined areas of Massachusetts and Connecticut, or of New Jersey and Connecticut.

If this great tract of land were fertile, or outside the arid region, it would not be an Indian reservation. As it is, the sunshine, temperate climate, and grandeur of scenery, constitute nearly all the measures of value the region now possesses. The Tunicha range of mountains cuts the country in two from the northwest to the southeast, and the Cariza spurs to the north add to its mountain area; the range and the spurs attaining an altitude of from 8,000 to 9,500 feet. Outside the mountain districts there are broad mesas, or table lands, and great valleys; the mountain sides being covered with growths of pine, cedar and spruce. The northern portions of the Navajo land, especially in the high or mountain altitudes, is cold in winter and cool in summer; while the lower portion is extremely hot in summer, and mild in winter. The migratory habits of the Navajo enable him to conform easily to climatic conditions, and therefore he will usually be found in the most comfortable part of his domain in summer or in winter. The ranges break down toward the valleys and plains on either side, and are seamed with many canons, that give rise to numerous small streams. The canons furnish nearly all the tillable land in the mountain region, and the streams the water for the irrigation of crops.

This country was inhabited before the advent of the Navajos; and by a people of superior intelligence, and far more peaceful and civilized than their successors. The valleys produced means of subsistence, and that they were cultivated long before the coming of the Navajos is shown by the remains of ancient reservoirs and well-planned irrigating canals; the Navajos not yet having undertaken anything of this kind in as scientific or practical a manner as their predecessors. The canons were fertile, sheltered and watered, the great walls of sandstone affording opportunity to cut homes in the rock; or offering cliff-covered terraces upon which to build homes that were at once safe retreats from the elements and from enemies.

In this region we find many of the ancient cliff dwellings, relics of a mysterious race of men. The Navajo land is peculiarly rich in these monuments of a lost people; a large number of the more remarkable ruins being found in the central part of the reservation. The modern Indian has no traditions to enlighten us as to the kind of people who preceded him in the occupation of that country, and who lived in the great communal houses that line the canons; neither stories nor legends that throw any light upon the time these Cliff Dwellers lived, or tell us who or what they were. He is but little interested in these ruins of the homes of people who were gone centuries before Columbus embarked upon unknown seas to find a new world, and pays scarcely more attention to them than to the rocks upon which they stand, or to the cliffs that rise above them like silent sentinels keeping guard over the deserted homes of a race whose work throws only a dim shadow upon the mists of antiquity.

That the Cliff Dwellers had disappeared long before the advent of the Navajos is also quite evident. If the latter had found the Cliff Dwellers occupying that field, there would have been war for supremacy, and the story of battle would have been handed down for many generations; legends of war being the most enduring of any subject with which an Indian mind has to deal.

Moreover the relics of these prehistoric people are evidence that they were much further advanced in the domestic arts than even the Navajos of the present time. It is not the nature of man, even savage man, to retrograde, and it would seem that the Cliff Dwellers had also advanced to a condition of peaceful life. The many implements of domestic use and of agriculture found in the ruins, and the absence of weapons of war, indicate this.

When white men first came in contact with the Navajos, they found them far behind the condition that had been attained by the Cliff Dwellers, as told by the mute eloquence of the work left behind by the earlier people. The Cliff Dwellers were weavers of cloth,

fine specimens of cotton weave having been found in the older ruins;
some in symbolical figures in colors that vie with the present Navajo
blanket. The Navajos did not learn to weave until comparatively
recent times; indeed, they did not spin a thread nor do any weaving until long after the occupation of the southwest by the Spaniards; and although they have dwelt in their present land for centuries, their period covers only a step backward toward the age in
which these prehistoric people of our southwest lived.

Major W. H. Emory, of the United States army, who appears
to have been the first American who visited this region of ruins
and intelligently observed and described them, said in his "Notes
of a Military Reconnoissance," under date October 28, 1846:

"Red cedar posts were found in many places, which seemed to
detract from their antiquity, but for the peculiarity of this climate,
where vegetable matter seems never to decay. In vain did we
search for some remnant which would enable us to connect the
inhabitants of these long deserted buildings with other races. No
mark of an edge tool could be found, and no remnant of any household or family utensils, except the fragments of pottery which were
everywhere strewed on the plain, and the rude corn-grinder still
used by the Indians. So great was the quantity of this pottery, and
the extent of ground covered by it, that I have formed the idea it
must have been used for pipes to convey water. There were about
the ruins quantities of the fragments of agate and obsidian, the
stone described by Prescott as that used by the Aztecs to cut out
the hearts of their victims. This valley was evidently once the
abode of busy, hard-working people. Who were they? Where
have they gone? Tradition among the Indians and Spaniards does
not reach them."

This Navajo country has been the home of the Indian so long,
that it is without doubt entitled to the distinction of presenting
evidence of the longest continuous occupancy by that race of any
portion of our territory; and therefore the land of the Navajo lends

interest to the story of the Navajo. A great portion of the Navajo country. was originally a vast table-land underlaid by deep strata of sandstone. The warring elements of thousands of years have grooved it with valleys, gorges and canons, leaving flat-topped mesas and perpendicular cliffs.

The wonderful Canon de Chelly is in the heart of the Navajo country; a deep, broad fissure in the table- and mountain-land, walled on both sides by great masses of red sandstone. The walls vary in height from twenty feet at the mouth, where the mountain- and table-land slope to the plain, to 800 feet where the canon penetrates the range. Within a distance of some twenty miles, which is nearly the length of the canon, there are about one hundred and fifty cliff-dwelling ruins. Several smaller canons diverging from the main one, notably the Canon del

FIGURE 5—* * "A Cliff Dweller's Sandal; upper and lower sides. More than 1,000 years old.

Muerto, and Monument Canon, also contain many ruins.

The pottery and other articles of domestic use found in the homes of these ancient people would indicate that they were the remote ancestors of the Pueblos; but how remote? "That's the question."

It is reported by very good authority that whole ears of carbonized Indian corn have been found embedded in lava; the lava-flow

containing this curious evidence of the long time ago of the Cliff
Dwellers having been later covered deep with debris. Charred roof
timbers with burned clay adhering to them, and many articles of
domestic life in close proximity, further indicated that these people
were there at the time of the last volcanic eruption in that country.
Calcined Indian corn has also been found on the floors of some of
the old dwellings, but having no ashes or cinders near to indicate
that it had been burned in an ordinary fire. The theory is becoming
popular that the grain was calcined by volcanic heat that raised the
temperature of the atmosphere above the scorching point, and
destroyed all life. Great basins, formerly the beds of lakes, are
now filled with lava, and ruins of the abodes of men are found at
the edge of these lava beds in such position that they appear to
have been at one time on the shores of the lakes.

What of the theory that a great population was destroyed suddenly by the fervent heat and poisonous fumes from molten lava?
The recent eruption of Mt. Pelee, and consequent destruction of
human life, helps us to believe it possible that the Cliff Dwellers
were destroyed in like manner. Implements of domestic utility are
found in great abundance, and which these people certainly would
have taken away with them if they had departed leisurely; while
the number of human remains discovered in and about the ruins
indicate a great and sudden fatality. Many writers have advanced
the theory that they were driven away by more warlike tribes, but
the skulls show no evidence that the people were killed in battle.
That was the age of the war club, and stone battle axe, and if the
people were slain by enemies, there would be many crushed skulls
among the remains; yet, as a matter of fact, a broken skull is
rarely seen.

It is probable that no single agency was responsible for the
abandonment of this region by these strange people. We can
readily believe that the land was once very fertile, and that a gradual
change from humid to arid conditions shortened the food supply,

and that this, together with increasing numbers, compelled many to abandon their homes and seek productive valleys to the south; and that subsequent great convulsions of nature causing volcanic eruptions completed the work. These would be followed by a long period of desolation; and thousands of years may have elapsed between the departure of the Cliff Dwellers and the restoration of that region to conditions fit for the habitations of man. Gradually the country recovered, and the soil, enriched by a long period of rest, stimulated the growth of grass, shrubs and trees; and finally the Navajo pilgrim from the north came in and took possession.

In the valleys, along the rivers, and near the foothills, but on level ground, we find a class of ruins that we must believe are older than the cliff dwellings. Great communal houses they were, some isolated, some in scattered village form, but each individual house presenting evidence of having sheltered a large community. We find in each living rooms, prison cells, and estufas or places of meeting and worship, and can still trace the canals that brought water from the river to each communal palace. There is evidence shown by old lines of irrigating canals and ditches, that the valley all around for miles was once cultivated by these people.

The more interesting of this class of ruins are found near Aztec, N. M. There is one principal ruin that commands the most attention. Many of the walls are still standing, at a height of forty feet above the level of the surrounding country. The walls average two and one-half feet in thickness, the outer and inner layers being of dressed stone, and the center filled in with cobble laid in mortar. As the pile appears now, it has a ground area of 300 by 400 feet, and judging from the heaps of debris around, it must have been a building 250 by 350 feet. Estimating the amount of debris that has fallen from the walls, and calculating how much of the present wall it would duplicate, we have a building seven stories high. The rooms remaining are small, and it is not guess-work to assign 100 to each story, or 700 rooms to this great communal palace.

Within a short distance are two more ruins of the same general character, but smaller.

The quarry from which the flat stones of the outer parts of the walls were brought is about three miles away. A wide trail from which the cobble-stones have been removed, can still be traced from the ruins to the quarry. As the Cliff Dwellers had no beasts of burden, nor mechanical means of transportation, the millions of pieces of stone required to build these great edifices must have been carried by men, women and children. Either great numbers enabled them to do the work in a few years, or it took generations of time to transport the material and complete such a pile of masonry; though it is not likely that any others than those of the single community that was to occupy it were engaged in its construction, which was such that each story could be occupied when finished. The walls are not all exactly alike in construction, and this suggests that different masters, at different periods, may have superintended the work, and therefore that perhaps a century elapsed between the beginning and the completion of the building. An interesting fact noted is that the beams forming the ceiling of each room, and supporting the adobe floor of the room above it, are of cypress, and not cedar as is generally believed. The cypress long since became extinct in that region. Cedar beams are found in similar buildings in the valleys, and also in those in the cliffs. Many of these are long, straight trunks from twelve to fifteen inches in diameter. But no cedars that would make such beams are now to be found in that country. Whether cypress or cedar, the trees from which these timbers were obtained must have grown either hundreds of miles away, or at a time when local climatic conditions were entirely different from what they now are.

But two of the rooms have been excavated, and in these a number of mummified skeletons were found, together with many pieces of pottery, and other relics of domestic life, such as beads, stone implements, needles and awls of bone. With relation to the mummified skeletons, it must not be inferred that they are anything like the mummies found in Egypt. In consequence of the dryness of the atmosphere, the bodies do not decay, but the flesh shrivels upon the bones, form and features in many instances being well preserved. As all these relics are found duplicated in the ruins of the cliff dwellings, there is little doubt that the older buildings were inhabited by the same race of people; and therefore it is fair to presume that these valley dwellers were driven from their homes and compelled to establish new and safer ones in the fastnesses of the canons and mountains because of the persecutions of hostile and more warlike tribes.

In that country well-informed people to-day call the valley dwellers "Aztecs," and the mountain or cliff people "Cliff Dwellers." Call them what we will, Aztecs, Cliff Dwellers, or Cave Dwellers, they were evidently of the same race. This is shown not only by the similarity of their relics, but by conformity in stature, and in form of skulls, of the remains of the people found in all the ruins.

People in other lands question the age of these buildings and relics on the score that they would long since have crumbled to dust if they were as old as claimed. But we must remember that many of these homes are chiseled from the solid rock. Others are built under overhanging cliffs and are never reached by a drop of moisture, while the remains of the valley communal houses are protected from the elements by heaps of debris. All are built at a great altitude, many of them more than a mile above the level of the sea; and in an atmosphere so rare and dry that it is in itself a preservative. In addition to these conditions, we must consider that it is an arid country where the rain fall is very slight. In such a climate and at such an altitude, there is seemingly no limit to the length of time a cedar beam, for instance, would be preserved if sheltered from the elements.

Of the age of these old communal buildings we can only guess. We know that they were crumbling in ruins long before Columbus landed on our shores, from the fact that some explorers and investigators in their excavations have discovered old foundations upon which later buildings, now in ruins, were erected. Therefore it is not difficult to believe that these people may have occupied that country even before the Chrisitan era.

We know the Cave, or Cliff Dweller is gone, and the Navajo is there occupying the same region, but absolutely refusing to live in any of the old houses, no matter if, as is sometimes the case, they are quite accessible and could easily be made far more comfortable than the rude huts in which he now lives. Many of the ruins have served as burial places for the Navajos for a long time. The Navajo burial cists are frequently found in them, some showing evidence of having been constructed many years ago. The Navajo burial cist is generaly a dome-shaped structure of stone, usually circular, although some of them are oblong in form, with a square hole left in the top for ceremonial purposes. The hole not being large enough to admit a human body, we infer that the body was laid on the ground and the cist or tomb built around and over it. Ruins favorably located are also used by the Navajos as granaries for the storage of wheat and corn, and as shelters for their flocks of sheep.

The Navajo land is an arid country. Excepting at higher altitudes in the mountain ranges, where the rainfall is greater, crops do not thrive without irrigation. There is evidence that the Cliff Dwellers cultivated a much greater area of the mesa and canon lands than is now tilled by the Navajos. That the former did not cultivate by irrigation all the available land is evident from the fact that the remains of irrigating ditches and reservoirs are not found in number and extent sufficient to have furnished water for all the land, under present conditions. It is possible that different climatic conditions then prevailed, and that there was sufficient rain to enable them to cultivate many tracts that are now entirely arid. If this were not the case, it is a wonder how the swarms of

FIGURE 6—A NAVAJO "SWEAT HOUSE"

people who once occupied the thousands of communal houses managed to exist.

To-day all the arable land in that country, even if supplied with irrigating ditches wherever water could be conveyed, would not support one-tenth the population that once flourished there. The relics of these ancient people indicate that they were not great hunters, but were of a rather peaceful nature, largely devoted to agricultural pursuits. Great quantities of corn are found in the ruins, and but little evidence of any means of subsistence excepting grains and fruits.

The Navajos have not made much of a success of their civil engineering, and the few irrigating canals they have are illy constructed and not laid out on approved lines. Wheat is grown to some extent, but the fields are small, and all the work of harvesting is by hand, the cutting being done with knives. Grain is threshed in the old way, by placing the sheaves on the ground inside an inclosure, and then turning in a flock of goats and driving them around over the sheaves until the grain is threshed out. It is winnowed by pouring it from a wide shallow willow basket, usually upon a blanket spread upon the ground. After winnowing, it is washed and then dried in the sun. There are two reasons for this: the first, to thoroughly clean it, and the second, to make it softer, so that it can be more easily ground by hand in the rude stone "metate," which is still used, as it has been used by the Indians of the southwest for hundreds of years, as the only means of grinding their grain. Indian corn of a small flinty variety is grown to some extent, but the cold nights and the high altitude are not favorable to successful corn culture.

The peach is their favorite fruit and practically the only one receiving very much attention. Peach trees were introduced into New Mexico by the Spaniards at an early day, and in every sheltered nook in the canons of the Navajo country, peach trees are found growing without culture, apparently in a wild state; but in fact young trees and peach pits were planted there by the Navajos. When the peaches ripen it is a holiday time in the Navajo land, and all who can be spared from tending the flocks gather at the orchards and gorge themselves with the lucious fruit, which reaches a high perfection of quality in these sunny gardens of Nature. The peach orgie continues until all the fruit is eaten; as none is taken away, nor preserved in the dried form.

They also grow apples, melons, squashes, pumpkins, onions and beans, all of which thrive remarkably well under irrigation. Irish potatoes are grown in the mountain regions and are of excellent quality. Wild cherries and plums, different species of wild currants and gooseberries, and wild blackberries and raspberries, flourish to some extent. The fruits do not appear to receive any attention in the way of cultivation, further than to plant the trees or seeds, which are then left to do the best they can.

In spite of this, magnificent crops of peaches and apples are grown, the soil in the canons seeming just fitted for them, there being sufficient moisture there to bring them to perfection; while the climate and bright sunshine combine to make the Navajo fruits of delicious quality.

The Navajo land is a mountain, mesa and valley country (Figure 4), with the mountains predominating. A country of cliffs and canons, presenting many difficulties to travel, which is almost entirely over narrow trails, either on foot or horseback. Of the rock formation, the most conspicuous is the bright red sandstone that the elements have carved into many irregular and picturesque shapes. Often in the distance a mass of rock will appear like a house or castle, and sometimes a spire, reaching high above the surrounding rocks, seems to be surmounting a cathedral. These scenes occur so often and appear so vividly real that they will forever remain a striking feature of the magnificent landscape that makes the Navajo land a marvel of scenic beauty and grandeur.

THE NAVAJO

FIGURE 7—* * "he struts and poses in great style until he scents his mother-in-law"

THE Navajo has long been a conspicuous figure among the Indians of our southwest. Strong, and made self-reliant by many years of successful warring upon neighboring tribes, he had become imbued with his own importance, and therefore held aloof from the advances of the white man until long after nearly all the neighboring tribes had laid down their arms. He was among the last to leave the war-path of offense or defense, and finally, when conquered, was among the first to become self-supporting; though he still retains much of his wild nature, and has absorbed fewer of the white man's vices than have the adjacent tribes.

The Navajos are descended from the great Athabascan family of Indians which formerly occupied a large portion of British America. The word "Navajo" was derived from the Spanish "Navajoa," applied to a district on the San Juan and Little Colorado rivers; and as the Navajos occupied that region, the Spaniards styled them "Apaches de Navajoa." They were not for from right in claiming them as Apaches, as there is good authority for saying that the latter were descended from the same Athabascan stock. The Navajos, however, do not recognize the name thus applied to them, but call themselves Tinnai or Tinneh, meaning "the people."

Some authorities claim that these people entered their present country in the Thirteenth Century, while others say they came in the Fourteenth or the Fifteenth Century; but there seems to be no basis but that of speculation upon which to attempt to determine the period of their coming. The home of the Athabascans was far to the north, and it is likely that by slow movement the Navajos traveled south by easy stages, along the eastern ranges of the Rocky Mountain region until they reached the great area of mountains and plains in southern Colorado and Utah, and in northern New Mexico and Arizona, in which they established themselves.

They have may mythical stories of their origin. One is to the effect that they came across a narrow sea beyond the setting sun, and landed on the northern shore of this country. There they were persecuted by enemies, and finally, in desperate straits, invoked the Great Spirit, who sent them a great ship of rock upon which they were safely carried high in air, and brought to their present land.

The "ship rock" of the Navajos is known to all travelers in the southwest. Rising from a level plain, about thirty miles west from Farmington, New Meixco, it stands out in strong relief from whatever direction it may be viewed, and in its weird loneliness and grandeur seems a fitting subject for an Indian legend. The Navajos consider the rock sacred.

Another story is that the ancestors of the Navajo tribe were brought from the far north on the back of a great bird; and still another, that they came up from the center of the earth. Their legends differ as to the means of transportation, but, with the exception of the idea that they came up out of the earth, they generally agree that they came from the far north. The most acceptable of their stories is that they were guided by a messenger from the sky, and after a long journey, and much suffering at the hands of enemies they met on the way, they were finally directed to their present country. There is also a vague tradition among them that

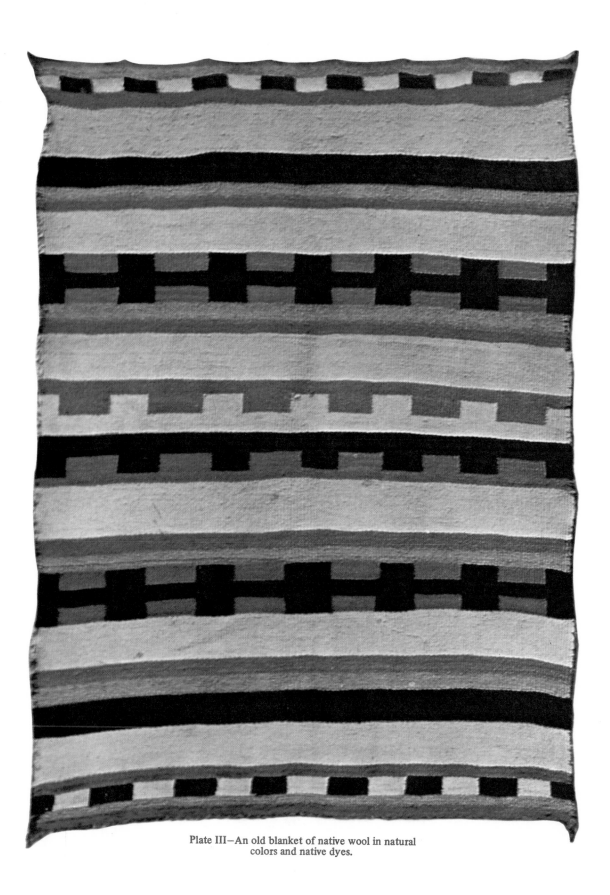

Plate III—An old blanket of native wool in natural
colors and native dyes.

they came by water. But, about the only things we certainly know of their history is their Athabascan origin, and that they have been in our southwest for a long time.

The Navajos are much attached to the region in which they live, and often refer to it as "our Mother land." They tell us that the Apaches were once Navajos, and that they came "long time ago," before the time of four old men—ancestors of the present Navajos—father, grandfather, great-grandfather, great-great-grandfather; and to this they add another story that "long time ago" whole bands of Pueblos ran away from the Spaniards and joined their people. They also tell that the Cliff Dwellers were carried away by a "bad wind" long before the Navajos arrived; which is probably a mere attempt of theirs to account for the deserted and ruined buildings.

The land was not entirely the Navajos' ideal, the climate being far milder than that of their original home in the north. Shelter, mountains, water and pasture were there, but at the time of their arrival pasture was not of direct value to them. Wild game was not as plentiful as farther north, and there was much arid land. We do not know why they concluded to occupy such a country, but it is probable that, expecting to find a better region, one better suited to them, by going farther, they were halted in their march south by the power of numbers of the Pueblos, whose northern borders they had invaded.

At this time the Navajos were not a great Indian nation. The tribe was small and, from the best evidence we can now obtain, was not of a warlike disposition. They were not noted for success in hunting wild game, and subsisted very largely upon nuts and roots, clothing themselves with the skins of such animals as they killed. They soon began to receive recruits from the Apaches, and other neighboring tribes, which accounts for their present composite or mixed character as a race; but prior to 1680, they were not strong enough to engage in anything but a predatory warfare with neighboring tribes. They have always been known as "field" or "plains" Indians, to distinguish them from the habitually sedentary tribes, like the Pueblos.

The industries of an aboriginal people are shaped by their surroundings and the character of the country in which they live. The climate, soil, forests or plains, adaptability for agriculture, and game for the chase, all help to determine how they can best sustain life; and when this is decided, their habits will be found to reflect their environment.

The Navajos are sedentary only to the extent that they have for a long time occupied about the same region. Within this immense area, they have been restless, wandering shepherds, without permanently fixed habitations. Soon after 1662, by pillage or barter, they secured a few sheep from the Pueblos who, in turn, had obtained them from the Spaniards. This acquisition had much to do with changing their mode of living; and as they learned the art of weaving, it marked the beginning of an important epoch in their tribal history.

The Navajo country is not adapted to extensive agricultural operations, and probably was not well supplied with game even in the earlier times; but if it had been, it would not have taken many years for its new occupants to destroy the wild animals to the extent, at least, of making them a precarious dependence as a source of food supply. The climate demanded clothing far beyond the supply of the skins of wild animals, and some industry had to be found suited to their environment, or the people must migrate again.

Fortunately, the pasture land helped them to solve the problem, and the Navajos turned out to be good shepherds. Their flocks increased until, for a number of years, they have counted a half million sheep as their own. This influenced their destiny, and has transformed them from fierce marauders into comparatively peaceful pastoral people. Nearly every family owns a flock of sheep and goats; the flesh of the latter being more generally used

FIGURE 8—NAVAJOS WORSHIPING THE ELEMENTS
(*From the painting by F. P. Sauerwen*)

for food than that of the sheep. With a population of 20,000, their herds would have an average of twenty-five sheep to every man, woman and child. The tendency of the flockmaster of the west is toward wealth, and the Navajos have proceeded far enough in that direction as to be beyond want, while many of them are rich. It is to be remembered that what would be good pasture land in the Navajo country, would be thought barren waste in the east, or in other lower altitudes. It requires about six acres to feed properly a single Navajo sheep, and as water is scarce and found only at long intervals, the shepherd must keep his flocks moving constantly.

The whole family moves with the sheep, and lives practically out of doors; or, at best, in hastily constructed shelters made by throwing up a circle of brush, and covering it, or not, as material may or may not be at hand. These changes from one pasturage to another, often take a family over hundreds of miles, and during this migratory life the spinning and weaving go on, the simple machinery required for the industry being a part of every camping equipment. As winter approaches, they turn toward sheltered places, but may or may not return to the abode of the previous winter.

In a particularly rich region well supplied with water, a number of families will remain in close proximity to one another, but they are usually held together by family ties, rather than by a community of interests. It is a singular fact that, notwithstanding accessions from the Pueblos, who were essentially village Indians, there are no villages of Navajos. Their dwellings are not built in conspicuous places, but seem to be located rather with a view to concealment. The springs, rivers and other watering places, are by the tribal laws considered common or public property, but tillable lands are subject to individual ownership; such ownership, however, is established only by priority of occupation, and can be retained only so long as the land is being tilled.

The Navajos are communal in their form of government and customs, particularly as relates to the grazing lands, which are, as a general rule, common property; and the cutting of timber, or use of water, and the harvesting of peaches or wild fruits that grow in the canons are not restricted on account of any individual claims of ownership. There is a head chief, who owes his position to election; but, with one exception, none of these chiefs has ever achieved great fame as a leader in warfare, or great reputation as a wise or sagacious ruler; and none has stood out as a prominent figure in war or peace. The exception, and the only one of whom we have a record, who made a reputation among his people as a wise ruler, was Manuelito, born in 1821, elected chief in 1850, and who served until his death in 1894. His rule was of an advisory nature, rather than arbitrary, which no doubt accounted for his popularity while living.

There are many sub-chiefs, whose jurisdictions extend over only small areas of tribal territory; and upon them devolves the local execution of the few lightly-resting tribal laws they have. These executives do not occupy their positions by hereditary right; neither are they always elected. Oftentimes, in consequence of superior intelligence or tact, thy grow into their places, as it were, and their influence is, as a rule, in proportion to their ability as diplomats. The usual method of "appeal" from the unsatisfactory ruling of a local chief is by disregarding it, and there is no court by which he can compel obedience.

The Navajos have some little industries, aside from their general one of blanket-weaving. The women knit stockings, using four needles in much the same manner as the whites, but do not seem to be able to learn to form the heel or toe. Although the knitting needles they now use are procured from the whites, they are no evidence that the Navajos learned the art of using them from the whites, as we find knitted leggings made from human hair or the fibre of the yucca, as well as the bone and wooden

needles used in making them, in the ruins of the cliff dwellings
in the Navajo land.   The Pueblo women, from whom the Navajos
learned blanket-weaving, were also knitters.   The Navajo women
are quite skilful basket-makers, but confine their work principally
to sacred baskets used in the marriage and other ceremonies. Only
the old women, who are familiar with the rites of the medicine
men make these baskets.

Baskets needed for domestic use are procured by barter
from their neighbors, the Apaches, who are skillful basket-makers;
and in like manner, they procure pottery from the Pueblo Indians.
The Navajos are expert in tanning buckskin and making it into
moccasins, leggings and other garments, but the bead work on
these articles is done by the Utes, who also tan buckskin and make a
great variety of ornamental bead work.

The principal tribes of the southwest, the Navajos, Apaches,
Utes, and Pueblos, are each celebrated for some form of handi-
craft, and as one does not encroach upon the work of the other,
it leads to much trading between the tribes, each desiring to possess
articles made by the others (Figure 9.)   The Navajos weave
blankets and make ornaments of silver.   Each of the four divisions
of the Apache tribe—the Mescalero, Pima, Jacarilla and San Carlos
Apaches, makes baskets, differing slightly, but strongly characteristic.   It is only a few years since the Shoshone Indians, of Idaho
and Utah, made long pilgrimages to the south for the purpose of
trading with the Navajos, the Shoshones being celebrated for their
fine buckskin garments and other articles, beautifully ornamented
with beadwork.

In late years many fine blankets of Navajo weaving, from
twenty to forty years old, have been found among the Shoshones
of Idaho and Utah.   Mrs. A. L. Cook, of Pocatello, Idaho, has a
good collection gathered in that vicinity, which the Shoshones
probably could not have procured in any other way than by barter
with the Navajos.

The Pueblo women are celebrated for pottery of rough, highly ornamented, and unique patterns. In this work they are artists; the scrolls and figures with which their pottery is decorated, nearly all being symbolical, and to a great extent form the basis of Navajo symbols and patterns.

The Navajo is not a lazy Indian, but is willing to work at anything remunerative; and in this he is an exception among red men generally. He herds sheep and cattle, and does all the farm work, and is ready to serve the white man at any kind of labor. He is also a silversmith, and is quite skilful in hammering and engraving buttons, buckles and discs for belts. These latter are from three to four inches in diameter, and round or oval in form, roughly engraved, and of pure silver of value in weight of from one to two dollars each.

The early Spanish invaders found very skillful workers in metals among the Pueblo Indians. As we shall see later on that the Navajos learned the art of weaving from the Pueblo Indians, it is reasonable to assume that their first knowledge of working in metal came from the same source. The Pueblo Indian, on account of his permanent abode, has better facilities than the Navajo, but in spite of his disadvantages, the latter is the most skillful.

The Navajos' metal-working equipment consists of a rude and temporarily constructed forge, charcoal, crucibles of clay, molds of clay or sandstone, a blow-pipe, tongs, and such requisites as he can get at the trading posts—emery paper, files, and so forth. The anvil is any piece of iron of sufficient weight that he can find—a piece of railroad rail, or the butt of an ax, a wedge, or a heavy bolt. One of Goodman's photographs (Figure 10) shows a Navajo silversmith at work, and illustrates the crude facilities he has at hand.

Belts and necklaces of silver are their pride, and are worn more by the men than by the squaws. The material used is either Mexican or American silver dollars, or bars of silver which they procure from the traders. They are so skillful and patient in hammering and shaping that a fairly good-shaped teaspoon is often made of a silver dollar without melting and casting. As they are able to procure and learn to use better facilities, their work is growing better; the ornaments they make now being superior to those made a dozen years ago. Some of their patterns are beautiful, though

FIGURE 9—NAVAJO INDIANS TRADING
(*From the painting of F. P. Sauerwen*)

entirely original. One buckle in my collection, so far as artistic design is concerned, might have been made by Tiffany. Weaving is, however, their principal and most attractive industry.

The Navajos should give their women credit for the wide and distinctive reputation their tribe has achieved solely from the Navajo blanket. Possibly the men are willing to concede this, which would largely account for the social independence of the

Navajo squaw as compared with the women of adjacent tribes. She certainly occupies a higher plane than is common among women of the North American Indians.

The Navajos have many songs illustrating their tribal myths. Songs for the storm, rain and wind; songs of peace and war; songs of love and hatred, joy and sorrow. Strangely enough the Navajo women do not join in any of the songs. Her neighbors, the Pueblo women, sing with the men in songs of ceremony; and the "Metate," or corn-grinding, song of the Zuni women, is peculiarly weird and musical. The Navajo woman is songless: her art being spinning and weaving, to which she devotes her life. Silently, almost sadly, but all the while devotedly, she toils, and is an example of patient industry and love for the work in which she is engaged.

The Navajos have a few fetiches or talismans, supposed to possess mysterious power, and to be the habitations of deities from which aid may be expected. These are generally represented by an animal; the horse and sheep being prominent as such fetiches. The horse fetich is carved from white limestone, and usually the work is done by a medicine man. It is carried in a medicine bag on occasions of the hunt, or of any important undertaking or journey, and as they depend upon the endurance of their horses in nearly everything they udertake, this fetich is to insure the strength of the animal. The sheep fetich is carved from white spar, and usually is finished with eyes of turquoise. These are carried by the shepherds to insure the fecundity of their flocks, to protect them against disease, and guard them against animals of prey. These two charms cover the most important two possessions of the Navajos—the horse and the sheep, and are the only ones now in use of which I have any certain evidence.

The Navajos have many superstitions, and believe in witchcraft, and that sickness and death are caused by a "Chinde" or devil. The antidote for witchery is singing and drumming over the patient by friends or relatives, and if this does not effect a cure, the "Shaman" or medicine man is called in. They believe that at the ends of a rainbow they will find messages from the Great Spirit; and anything bright and beautiful, is to them a harbinger of good.

Early travelers in the Navajo land detail the story of an old Navajo sorcerer, or wizard, who, having been suspected of practicing the "black art," confessed it, seemed proud of his pretended powers, and told his people that by charms of human hair and flesh, powdered wolves' teeth, and dried and powdered lizards, he could destroy the whole Navajo nation. He was tied, shot with arrows, and asked why he did not kill his captors; but he died without having injured any of them. He was probably a crazy old man, and because of his delusions was murdered by his superstitious people.

The Navajo goddess is "Assunnutli" (the woman in the sea). This goddess is reputed to be of double sex, and has dispensed many favors to the Navajos; having, among other gracious acts, sent blue corn to the men, and white corn to the women. When property is stolen they sing to "Assunnutli" to ascertain the identity of the culprit.

Like all Indians, the Navajos are inveterate gamblers, and will wager everything they possess, even to the clothing on their backs. They are fond of foot-racing and wrestling, and horse-racing is also very popular with them.

Not being the most mighty of modern Nimrods in the chase, a favorite hunting plan of the Navajos is to build two long converging lines of brush and stones, ending at an enclosure, into which the animals are driven to be slaughtered. All animals of prey are killed, but in case of game animals, such as antelope, or deer, some are allowed to escape, partly on account of superstition, and partly to avoid exterminating a valuable food supply.

To the Navajos the bear is a sacred animal, and probably became so in the early years when they had no weapons with which to successfully combat him; the idea of sacredness arising from the ability of the bear to win in battle with them. A respect for strength and invulnerability, rather than regard for sacred things, may thus have given Bruin a place among their deities.

They will not catch nor eat fish. When the white men first invaded their country they found the mountain streams fairly alive with trout, which would not have been the case if the Indians had desired them for food; as they had sufficient cunning to have depleted the streams if they had so used fish. They believe that the spirits of their dead enter into the fish, and are fond of relating the fable that "long time ago" their people killed a great number of their enemies in battle and threw the bodies into the river, and that the bodies turned into fish.

Believing that the wind gives them life, they often go at night to some high place during a storm and there worship the elements (Figure 8). The heavy rain they call the male rain, and the light rain the female rain; believing both to be necessary for the proper maturing of their crops.

The Navajos have a horror of the dead, as well as of any habitation in which a person has died; and as many of the old cliff ruins contain the remains of the people who once lived in them, they will not under any circumstances use them as a place of residence. The nearest they come to this is that oftentimes they carry away stones from the ruins to be used in building dwellings for themselves.

From the Conquest of Mexico, up to 1821, the land of the Navajos was a part of the Spanish territory. In 1821 the people of Mexico threw off the Spanish yoke and established an independent government. Beginning about the year 1750, and during all the subsequent time of the Spanish and the Mexican rule, the Navajos were on the war-path. They made frequent raids into the country south of them and occupied by the Pueblo Indians and Mexicans, and ran off cattle, sheep and horses, and carried away such grain and forage as they could transport. In retaliation, the

Mexicans made many counter expeditions into the Navajo country, which became the scene of continual warfare.

Lieutenant Pike, writing from New Mexico in 1808, in speaking of the "Nanahaws" (Navajos), states: "The Nanahaws are situated to the northwest of Santa Fe, and are frequently at war with the Spaniards. They are supposed to be two thousand warriors strong, and are armed with bows and arrows and lances. This nation, as well as all others to the west of them bordering on California, speak the language of the Apaches and Lee Panis, who are in a line with them to the Atlantic."

Major Emory, in his "Notes of a Military Reconnoissance" in the summer of 1846, writes as follows of Las Vegas, New Mexico:

"The village, at a short distance, looked like an extensive brick-kiln. Approaching, its outline presented a square with some arrangements for defense. Into this square the inhabitants are sometimes compelled to retreat, with all their stock, to avoid the attacks of the Eutaws [Utes] and Navajos, who pounce upon them and carry off their women, children and cattle. Only a few days since, they made a descent on the town and carried off 120 sheep and other stock. As Captain Cooke passed through the town ten days since, a murder had just been committed on these helpless people."

Major Emory quotes the address made by Colonel Kearney to the Mexicans at Santa Fe, August 15, 1846, which was as follows:

"Mr. Alcalde, and people of New Mexico: I have come amongst you by the orders of my government, to take possession of your country, and extend over it the laws of the United States. We consider it, and have done so for some time, a part of the territory of the United States. We come amongst you as friends—not as enemies; as protectors—not as conquerors. We come among you for your benefit—not for your injury. Henceforth I absolve you from all allegiance to the Mexican government, and from all obedience to General Armijo. He is no longer your governor. (Great sensation.) I am your governor. I shall not expect you to take up arms and follow me, to fight your own people, who may oppose me; but I now tell you, that those who remain peaceably at home, attending to their crops and their herds, shall be protected by me, in their property, their persons, and their religion; and not a pepper, not an onion, shall be disturbed or taken by my troops, without pay, or by the consent of the owner. But listen! He who promises to be quiet, and is found in arms against me, I will hang.

"From the Mexican government you have never received protection. The Apaches and the Navajos come down from the mountains and carry off your sheep, and even your women, whenever they please. My government will correct all this. It will keep off the Indians, protect you in your persons and property; and, I repeat again, will protect you in your religion. I know you are all great Catholics; that some of your priests have told you all sorts of stories—that we should ill-treat your women, and brand them on the cheek as you do your mules on the hip. It is all false. My government respects your religion as much as the Protestant religion, and allows each man to worship his Creator as his heart tells him is best. Its laws protect the Catholic as well as the Protestant; the weak as well as the strong; the poor as well as the rich. I am not a Catholic myself—I was not brought up in that faith; but, at least one-third of my army are Catholics, and I respect a good Catholic as much as a good Protestant.

"There goes my army—you see but a small portion of it; there are many more behind—resistance is useless."

This was upon the first entrance into Santa Fe by the United States troops. On September 30, 1846, writing of the mountain country northwest of Santa Fe, Major Emory says:

FIGURE 10—A NAVAJO SILVERSMITH

Plate IV—A curious and rare old blanket of sacred significance,
woven about 1845.

"I saw here the hiding places of the Navajos, who, when few in numbers, wait for the night to descend upon the valley and carry off the fruit, sheep, women and children of the Mexicans. When in numbers, they come in day-time and levy their dues. Their retreats and caverns are at a distance to the west, in high and inaccessible mountains, where troops of the United States will find great difficulty in overtaking and subduing them, but where the Mexicans have never thought of penetrating. The Navajos may be termed the lords of New Mexico. Few in number, disdaining the cultivation of the soil, and even the rearing of cattle, they draw all their supplies from the valley of the Del Norte."

This conditon continued, and for many years after the United States government became dominant in New Mexico and Arizona the Navajos persisted in their depredations, robbing and plundering from the Mexicans and Pueblos, and from our own people as well. An expedition was organized in 1863 under the direction of Kit Carson, which was successful in capturing the Navajo leaders and compelling a general surrender. The prisoners were then taken under military guard to Fort Sumner, New Mexico, where they were held until 1867, when, upon their promise to be good, they were returned to their old home, the present Navajo reservation.

At that time there were about 8,000 in captivity, but this number did not, however, represent the full strength of the nation. Many had hidden in the fastnesses of the mountains, and others had deserted to other tribes rather than go as prisoners of war to Fort Sumner. As near as can be ascertained, they numbered at that time about 13,000 all told, but they have since steadily increased, and now aggregate somewhere near 20,000. Upon their return to the reservation the government paid them four annuities, and in 1869 distributed among them a large number of sheep and goats. Since that time they have been self-supporting, excepting in the winter of 1894-95, when, on account of a severe drought in the preceding summer, their crops had failed, and therefore the government had to distribute sufficient rations to prevent suffering.

The Navajo is quite free from the signs of physical degeneracy so apparent in neighboring tribes. He is a robust Indian, but his type is not a fixed one. While his remote ancestors were of Athabascan stock, and much of the stalwart figure of the true Navajo is traceable to that origin, the numerous accessions from other tribes of differing physical contour, have produced a decidedly composite physical condition which is noticeable in difference of stature, in facial characteristics, and in general personal appearance among different members of the tribe. It is likely that this mixture of the blood of various adjacent tribes with that of the original Navajos, has had much to do in bringing about their present superior physical and mental condition as compared with other tribes in that region. As a rule, they are intelligent above the average North American Indian, which is demonstrated by the advantage they have taken of really unfavorable conditions to become independent of help from the government and, in a way, to become rich.

Their marital relations are peculiar to themselves, and a Navajo may take, not as many wives as he can support, but as many as he can manage; and having reached this limit, the wives do much toward supporting the husband. The men are the herders of the sheep and cattle, hunt wild game, build the dwellings and, as a rule, till what little land is cultivated.

The lineage of the Navajo is traced through the female line. The woman may, and often does, own the flocks of sheep, and as owner of the home her word is law in all that pertains to domestic affairs. She must, however, prepare the family meals, bring the wood and water, and work all her spare time at spinning and weaving. She has absolute control of her children, and her husband may not even discipline them without authority from her to do so. The only exception to her authority over the affairs of her offsping is when a daughter reaches marriageable age, when the bargain or sale to a suitor for her hand must be made with the father. If, upon trial, a wife proves unsatisfactory, and the husband cannot bring about a trade with another Indian who is in the same trouble, he may return the wife to her parents; but the purchase price need not be returned to the dissatisfied husband. The women do not consider this an indignity. If a Navajo woman is fond of her husband, her conduct is usually such as to merit his approval; but it is quite likely that if she rebels, or becomes unsatisfactory, it is because she wishes to be traded to some one she likes better, or returned to her home to await a new matrimonial venture.

Their food is of the simplest. The meat most generally used is mutton and the flesh of the goat, which are stewed; a pot for the evening meal being kept on the fire most of the day. This, with bread and coffee, constitutes the supper, with the exception that when pumpkins, potatoes or onions are in supply, they are usually stewed with the meat. They have no tables nor chairs, the stew being placed on the earthen floor in a big dish, where the family gathers around it, taking out the food with the fingers. They always eat everything in sight; nothing is left, no matter how much is cooked. As a rule there are only two regular meals, breakfast and supper; the breakfast being the simpler meal of the two. If meat is used at all for breakfast, it is fried in a skillet, and eaten with bread and coffee.

Even the permanent dwellings are almost devoid of furniture —without tables, chairs or bedsteads. They have plenty of blankets and undressed sheepskins, and when an Indian gets sleepy he rolls himself in a blanket and lies down upon the floor anywhere that suits him best. They do not use pillows. The only article of furniture common in all Indian homes of the southwest is a pole suspended from the ceiling along one side of the room, which does duty as a wardrobe.

As relates to dress, the woman is the more barbaric in her fancy. Gaudy calicos and bright red woolen cloths are used for skirts which, with sashes or belts of bright color, beads, silver and copper ornaments, and fancy beaded moccasins and leggings, constitute her chief desires; and in these, she dresses herself as occasion may require. The working dress of a squaw is usually a loose, ill-fitting garment of calico reaching to the knees; the legs and feet being incased in buckskin leggings and moccasins without ornamentation. She cares nothing for a head-dress of any kind, excepting a careless arrangement of the long, thick, jet-black hair Nature gave her, which is parted in the middle, and either allowed to hang at will, or gathered or tied in a knot, or made into a long braid.

The marriage ceremony seems to have no fixed form, the rite usually consisting of eating in some manner, and is quite simple. Sometimes a cake or loaf, prepared by the medicine man, is placed on the ground, and at other times a pudding is used; either of which the medicine man marks off in lines and spaces, for a reason we do not understand. The prospective bride and groom are seated beside the food, and at a signal they eat—the man beginning and the woman following—taking the food from along the lines marked out. When the circuit of the cake, or loaf, or pudding, is completed, they stand up and are pronounced man and wife. After the ceremony the squaws prepare a feast, and singing and dancing are kept up until all are tired out. In some instances the medicine man pours water upon the hands of the bride and groom just before eating begins, and at other times they go together to a spring or stream and wash each other's hands prior to the ceremony of eating. There are other unimportant variations in the ceremony, but the above will convey a general idea of the marriage rite.

An unfortunate feature of Navajo domestic life is the common aversion of the husband to the wife's mother, but there is no mother-in-law interference in domestic affairs. After marriage the husband will not look at or speak to his mother-in-law, and must have no communication with her under penalty of some blight upon his life. They believe that if a husband gazes upon his mother-in-law he will lose his eyesight, or that some other terrible calamity will happen to him. It is the duty of the mother-in-law to announce her approach, so that the husband can conceal himself until she has gone.

The case of Pablo, a Navajo singer, whose picture appears in Figure 7, is a present example in point. He puts on his best and struts and poses in great style until he scents his mother-in-law, when he disappears into hiding, a sneaking coward until she is gone.

As the Navajo is polygamous, it is possible that this singular custom originated in a theory of protection for the husband. A man with half a dozen wives would have as many mothers-in-law, and, according to beliefs prevalent among white people, would also have a pretty hard time if all of them exercised influence over his household. Therefore such a custom may be a very grave necessity in Navajo land.

HABITATIONS

FIGURE 11—* * "may be almost anything that can be considered a shelter"

THE habitations of a primitive people are of especial interest because they are always typical; each order of rough architecture being in harmony with the type of man who built it, and in keeping with his manner of life. As in influencing his industries, climatic conditions, the general character of the land on which he lives, mountains, plains, or forests, will modify to some extent his methods of providing shelter. But as a rule, the changes will not show marked departure from the general type evolved and long followed by a primitive tribe of people, unless there has been something like a revolution in modes of living.

Such a revolution befell the Navajos, and brought about a corresponding change in the forms of their abodes. As already related, prior to the time that they became possessed of sheep, cattle and horses they lived in the open field, and as plunderers of their neighbors. In no sense an agricultural people and without fixed habitations in that period of their career, the change from a condition of continued nomadic warfare to that of a pastoral life, was a very great one.

The Navajo is not a dweller in tents, wigwams or tepees, as we know these forms of habitations. Long use of a word often leads to the belief that the word was coined because it so fitly described the object. We think a wigwam is named just right to describe that kind of a structure; long association of the word with the object having been the means of such perfect reconciliation. The Navajo house is a "hogan," and, although the name is a comparatively new word, it seems to fit. The original Navajo word is "qugan," early converted into the popular name hogan, by which his home is known wherever the Navajo Indian is known. An expression made by a friend of mine when he first saw a Navajo home—"Well, it is a hogan, sure enough," illustrates the fitness of the name, which is applied to the two distinct forms, the winter and the summer hogan. From a little distance the winter hogan looks like a rough conical mound of earth, with an opening into darkness.

The Navajo hogan (Figure 12), at Putnam Springs, New Mexico, is typical of the winter habitation. The photograph was taken during a time of drought, when the structure was deserted; which accounts for the absence of a blanket from the doorway. This is an old hogan, showing many repairs by additions of branches of trees to secure the earth covering, and of the gnarled cedar trunks supporting the door-frame. Unsightly and unshapely as it may appear, it is built according to rule; a rule so rigid as to be almost a religious ceremony, and requiring every detail to be strictly carried out.

When a winter hogan is to be built the site is usually chosen in a secluded or sheltered spot; the choice always being such as will permit the door to face the east. The ground is leveled, and then a circle is drawn of the desired size; there being no general rule as to the diameter or height of a hogan. From about a foot inside this circle the ground is dug out to a depth of twelve or eighteen inches, and the bottom of this basin-like excavation is the floor of the hogan, to reach which a downward step or two must be taken; the foot or so of undisturbed soil left around it, and concentric with the circle, forming a circular seat or bench that encompasses the depressed floor. When this floor is smoothed and stamped until it is level and hard, the foundation is considered complete. Usually the builder of such a home calls to his assistance a number of his friends, and the building is completed in one day. Men are first sent out for the principal five timbers or poles. Each of three of these must be forked at one end, and of such shape as to firmly interlock when placed in position; the other two, sticks for the doorway, should be straight poles; all being trimmed and the bark taken off as a rough finish. The forked poles are laid on the ground, the forked ends together, and with the butts so arranged that each is outside the circle; one at the north, one at the west, and one at the south. The two straight poles are then laid with their butts to the east, and with the tops just inside the forks of the other three, and far enough apart to leave the desired space for the doorway. The timbers or poles used are usually from eight to twelve inches in diameter and from ten to twelve feet long.

In rearing the framework of the edifice, the three forked timbers are raised upright and then leaned toward the center until the forks lock. The poles for the doorway are placed at the same ground distance from the center as the others, and leaning inward and converging until their tops rest on each side of the apex; say, one foot apart at the top, and spreading to about four feet apart at the base, leaving an opening from the outer circle of the base to the center of the house. Two posts with forked tops are then planting upright between the door-poles at their base, standing about five feet high, and across these a lintel is placed in their forks; this arrangement forming the doorway, proper, over which a blanket is usually hung. The space between the top of this vertical door-frame and the leaning door-poles behind it, is levelly roofed over until it comes in contact with the two converging door-poles, and at the inward end of this bit of flat roof an opening is left through which smoke may escape. The sides of the structure are now filled in with smaller poles, the butts resting on the circle, with their tops reaching to the apex. After these poles are placed as closely together as possible, cedar boughs are woven in, and if convenient, the whole is covered with pine or cedar bark. The entire edifice is then further covered with earth to a depth of from four to eight inches, and the house is complete. A hogan from sixteen to eighteen feet in diameter averages about eight feet in interior height above the center of the floor.

FIGURE 12—A NAVAJO WINTER HOGAN

Colonel Cecil A. Deane writes me as follows concerning some hogans of peculiar form observed by him:

"The hogans I refer to I have seen only at one place, and I think they have never been described in government reports nor by any writer. On the little-traveled road leading in a southwesterly direction from the great ruins on the Charco to Gallup, N. M., about ten miles northeast of the Continental Divide, and thirty miles northeast of Gallup, we find a group of eight hogans at a place called Tigue (pronounced Togay). The peculiar location of these hogans is worthy of notice. At some remote period of time, a lake, comprising perhaps 2,000 acres, covered the present site of the hogans. Either because of the breaking of its retaining boundary, or because of evaporation, or both, the lake became dry, leaving a perfectly level surface—even now wholly devoid of vegetation. Near the east margin of the lake bed are numerous springs, a few of which discharge tepid water. Around each spring is found a circular deposit of dark sedimentary matter of perhaps three or four feet in height, which has been left by the overflowing waters, none of which is fit for use. Right in the midst of these miniature geysers, we find a large spring of clear, cold water, which is enclosed with walls of stone brought from the adjacent bluffs, and near it are the eight hogans I have referred to. They are circular in form, each about fifteen feet in diameter and eight feet at their greatest height. The walls are made of rough-dressed cedar or pinon logs, laid horizontally, having half-locking mortices at either end, and of such length as results in a nearly vertical wall to a height of about four feet, when their length is gradually reduced till the apex is reached, where an opening is left for the escape of smoke from the fire which burns in the center of the hogan. The doorway is, as in all instances, on the east side, which is closed by a blanket suspended from a horizontal lintel. The space between the logs is filled with small blocks of wood, and clay mortar, and the exterior surface is plastered with that material. No part of the floor is sunk below the general level, as I have observed in hogans of other types, and the obtuse angle formed where the walls meet the floor is used as a place of storage for the cooking utensils, blankets, etc., usually found in a Navajo home. When I visited these hogans in the spring of 1900, all were occupied, but I was informed through my interpreter, that the greatest number of their owners were more or less distant with their flocks of sheep or goats. As I was informed that this spring, which supplies water for the occupants of these hogans, is the only spring of living water within a radius of about fifty miles, we may reasonably infer that the permanency of the water is the cause of the permanent character of the hogans."

A Navajo summer hogan is a structure altogether different from the winter home, and may be almost anything (Figure 11) that can be considered a shelter. A circle of pine or cedar boughs, either planted in the earth or piled up three or four feet high, is one form. In this an opening is left in one side, the one most convenient, and without regard to points of the compass which are so important in the case of the winter hogan. In the center of this a fire is built, blankets are thrown over projecting branches for shade and cover, and in the enclosure the household labors and other duties are carried on. The family eat and sleep, the squaw sets up her loom, and weaving and other work go on just as regularly and as industriously as in the more pretentious home.

The house just described is the Navajos' rudest or simplest form of construction. There are degrees of betterment according to the length of time the shelter is expected to be used, or to the facilities or material at hand for construction. An excavation in a hillside, covered and sided with poles and brush, but with the entire front left open, is another form. Rough walls of stone, two or three feet high, arranged in a semi-circle and covered with any handy material is still another. A perpendicular wall of rock is sometimes utilized as a support for a "lean-to" constructed against it.

A rather picturesque summer hogan is the one shown in Figure 3, which is from a photograph by Goodman, of Bluff, Utah. It is simply a frame of small trees, with the front entirely open; the roof and three sides being lightly covered with branches of cottonwood and willow trees with the leaves left on them.

So the forms vary as conditions of occupation, location and materials vary, or as the industry or ingenuity of the builders differ. Occasionally a rich Navajo will build a hogan of logs or of rough stones laid up without mortar, and covered with timbers and earth; and he may also be ambitious enough to add a window, but if he does so it is never opened.

This form of winter hogan is shown in Figure 13. The picture clearly exhibits the method of construction, and also the forms of "Hostine" (Mr.) Joe, and the old medicine man who owns the outfit; the former on the left, and the latter on the right. So great a departure from the usual type of winter hogan is very modern, and is prompted by a desire to imitate the white man.

It will be noted that Navajo habitations are not, as a rule, of a very permanent character. A home that may be built and dedicated to use in a day, is not of great value, and may, for good reason, be abandoned at any time. For this, ill luck, sickness, or death may be sufficient cause, and therefore we find many deserted hogans that are in fairly good condition for occupation. As a strong superstition forbids further use of a hogan in which a person has died, often it is then destroyed; as no one of the tribe can be persuaded to enter it, much less live in it.

Of late years, if the owner of a hogan considers it of more than ordinary value, or is too lazy to construct a new one, he sees to it that the sick person is carried out, so that if he dies, he must die out of doors, and thus save the good reputation of the house.

Another quite common structure, and well distributed over the entire area of Navajo territory, is the "sweat-house." This is a miniature hogan, capable of accommodating only one person, who is required to take a lying or sitting position in it. It is freely used by the sick, and often by the well; and is one of the medicine man's "strong cards" for the cure of disease, and for the casting out of evil spirits. After stones have been heated and placed inside, the patient crawls in, the opening is closed, and he is soon in a profuse perspiration. When he has cooked long enough, he is taken out and rubbed dry with dry sand. The results as described by the Navajos are much the same as those from our more elaborate Turkish baths.

In Figure 6 is shown a sweathouse covered with a Navajo blanket to retain the heat better; the remains of the fire in which the stones were heated appearing in the foreground. A patient was inside undergoing the sweating ordeal when the photograph was taken; and to obtain the privilege of taking it Mr. Matteson was required to negotiate satisfactorily for a buckskin the attendant Indians desired to sell.

When a Navajo hogan has been completed, it must be dedicated by a ritual ceremony. The woman first clears the house of all rubbish accumulated in building, whereupon the husband builds a fire directly under the smoke hole. He then rubs the timbers with white corn meal, and also strews some of it in a circle around the fire, while repeating in slow, measured tones, the ritual of dedication. All the neighbors are then invited in and the ceremonial songs are sung, by which evil spirits are frightened away, and happiness, health and good luck invoked for the occupants.

As their hogans are not as a general rule built in the open, but concealed among the pines and cedars, or in the canons, no definite idea can be obtained of the population of the country by merely passing through it. In recent years the common Sibley tent has been used in summer to some extent, as it is less work to take it down, move and set it up again, than to build even the simplest summer hogan.

The medicine lodges are built much after the style of the hogans, but usually much larger. In these the medicine men live, and nearly all the ceremonial religious rites are celebrated in them. Most authorities agree that the Navajo is not a particularly religious Indian, for the reason, I suppose, that he does not make much ado about it. He has no public snake dances nor other ceremonies that are likely to attract the attention of a casual visitor; nor does he set up totem poles or idols in his public places. His only conspicu-

FIGURE 13—A MORE ELABORATE WINTER HOGAN

Plate V—A modern rug-blanket, made in 1891.

ous appliance of worship is the altar in the medicine lodge, which is hidden from the sight of white men, excepting those who are in very great favor .

These altars are fantastically ornamented with feathers, stalks and tassels of corn, grain, grasses and the like, and on the floor in front of the altar, are strewed strange symbols in colored sand— "sand paintings," as they are called by white folks; and over these the incantations are made, prayers are said and songs are sung, to invoke happiness, and success in their every undertaking.

Their songs of ceremony are according to long established rule, and are known only to the medicine men. The medicine men always demand pay for interceding with the gods, and a song or prayer commands a price commensurate with the importance of the case and of the assistance asked; and also with the ability of the applicant to pay. In this, as in many other things, our Navajo friend travels on lines parallel with those followed by many of his more enlightened white brethren.

Professor George H. Pepper relates that an old medicine man told him that he "often used colored clay and stones, but that they did no good—the patient only thought so; which was one way of saying that it was simply 'mind cure.' I was glad to hear this from an old medicine man of good standing, for it served to show how readily they would accept a new regime in the medicine world."

THE BEGINNING

FIGURE 14—* * "familiar landmarks today, but which were far more populous then than now"

THE Spaniards' thirst for gold stirred them to undertake the most hazardous and difficult adventures. They had conquered Mexico, laying waste the fair land of the Aztecs; and in doing so they disregarded all honorable rules of conquest. They burned and pillaged and murdered, until the admiration that was excited by their ambition and valor, was lost in the shame of the civilized world for the barbarous warfare they had waged against the peaceful and civilized Aztecs.

After they had established themselves in New Spain—the territory now known as Mexico—they began at once to plan explorations to regions of the north, about the wealth of which they had heard fabulous tales; and were particularly anxious to penetrate as far as the mythical Seven Cities of Cibola, having heard especially remarkable stories of their opulence.

The first expedition was that of Coronado in 1540, but was without any very important results. In 1582, General Espejo organized and led another expedition, and as early as 1600 the subjugation of the natives was practically completed, and the Spanish colonization of New Mexico had begun. The subjugated people were forcibly converted to the religion of the invaders, and then enslaved.

The Pueblo Indians' Great Deity was the God of Nature; their Creed, peace and harmony. The white man's God of Revelation brought to them the example of carnage, oppression and slavery; and they endured the indignities put upon them by inhuman masters, until even patient Pueblo human nature could endure it no longer. Among the traditions preserved by the present clans of this once numerous and powerful tribe, is one to the effect that the culminating cause of their ancestors' rebellion against their cruel enslavers was that several hundreds of their people had been smothered in mines in which they were compelled to work.

Lieutenant Pike's narrative of events in New Mexico, written while he was at Santa Fe in 1808, shows that the cruelties practiced by the Spaniards prior to the insurrection in 1680, were continued up to the time of his visit. The retribution he invoked came with the Mexican War:

"The civilized Indians of the Province of New Mexico consist of what were formerly twenty-four different bands, the several names of which I was not able to learn. But the Keres were one of the most powerful; they form at present the population of St. Domingo, St. Philip's and Deis, and one or two other towns. They are men of large stature, round, full visage, fine teeth, and appear to be of a gentle, tractable disposition; they resemble the Osage more than any nation in my knowledge. Although they are not the vassals of individuals, yet they may properly be termed the slaves of the state; for they are compelled to do military duty, drive mules, carry loads, or in fact perform any other act of duty or bondage that the will of the commandant of the district, or any passing military tyrant, chooses to ordain. I was myself eye-witness to a scene which made my heart bleed for these poor wretches at the same time that it excited my indignation and contempt, that they should suffer themselves with arms in their hands to be beaten and knocked about, by beings no ways their superiors, unless a small tint of complexion could be supposed to give that

superiority.   Before we arrived at Santa Fe, one night we rested
near one of the villages where resided the families of two of our
horsemen.   They took the liberty to pay them a visit in the night.
Next morning the whole were called up, and because they refused
to testify against their imprudent companions, several were knocked
down from their horses by the Spanish dragoons with the butt end
of their lances; yet with the blood streaking down their visage, and
arms in their hands, they stood cool and tranquil!   Not a frown,
not a word of discontent or palliation escaped their lips.   Yet, what
must have been the boiling indignation of their souls, at the insults
offered by the wretch, clothed with a little brief authority.   But
the day of retribution will come in thunder and in vengeance."

In the year 1675, under crafty leaders, the Pueblos began
plotting rebellion, and all the tribes in central and northern New
Mexico soon joined in the determination to drive the Spaniards
from their land.   From Pecos on the east to Moqui on the west,
from Taos on the north to Isleta on the south, the seeds of rebellion
were sown.   They took deep root in the hearts of the zealous
devotees of the religion of the Indian, and were stimulated by hatred
of the religion or Christianity of the Spaniards.   The villages of
Taos, San Ildelfonso, Isleta, Laguna, Acoma, Zuni and Moqui,
most of which are familiar landmarks to-day (Figure 14), but
which were far more populous then than now, all joined to free
their land from the hated Spaniards; and they were successful.

In the year 1680, their victory was made complete and not a
Spaniard was left alive in all their territory, over which Spanish
power had ruled so unwisely.

During that period of affliction the peaceful nature of the
Pueblos had greatly changed.   The reader will remember that in
all their narratives the Spaniards mention the Pueblos as "civilized"
Indians; even before they had succeeded in occupying their territory.   The white man had taught them the beauty of conquest and
carnage, and they had acquired the taste for human blood.

As the Spaniards retreated, the Indians first gave way to rejoicing; then to destroying everything that reminded them of Spanish rule. The churches were burned, as were all official documents relating to Spanish government, and the priests were subjected to great indignities. Their robes were worn in mockery, then torn to shreds and burned, that there might be no relic left of a religion that had been so closely associated with Pueblo misfortunes. Those of the tribe who had been baptized, were washed in public places, to cleanse them of what they thought to be evil influences. Then, being their own masters again, they were confronted with a problem more difficult than they had anticipated—the problem of self-government.

During the period of Spanish domination, such tribal laws as the Pueblos had had before the coming of the Spaniards had been almost forgotten by the old, while the young had never personally known them. Hating bitterly the laws and the rule which they had overthrown, freedom was accompanied by extremely diversified sentiments among the people, and therefore they soon found the problem of self-government a difficult one. An attempt was made to unite all the tribes under the direction of a single ruler, but there were, however, too many conflicting interests; too many village clans; too many ambitious chiefs; too many crafty, designing medicine men; and not sufficient knowledge of even the simplest tribal laws to stem the current of dissention that finally arose. They began fighting among themselves, and civil strife destroyed the power of numbers.

The Spaniards took advantage of the situation, and by 1694, just fourteen years after the insurrection, General Vargas had reconquered the whole field, and his people were again in full possession.

All this was in the interest of our friends, the Navajos, who had taken no part in the insurrection of 1675-80, and had not aided the Pueblos against the second coming of the Spaniards. As either the Pueblos or the Spaniards presented an unprotected point, they took advantage of it to rob and plunder, and in this way accumulated stores of food, secured many sheep, and grew stronger while the Pueblos were growing weaker. Upon the return of the Spaniards many Pueblos had joined the Navajos, preferring to become even Navajos rather than again to live under Spanish rule. The deserters from the Pueblos were in sufficient number to add materially to the strength of the Navajos, and from that date the latter began to rank as the most powerful of the southwestern Indian tribes.

In the foregoing some of the historical circumstances under which the art of weaving was introduced among the Navajos are outlined. Their first step toward it was in the acquisition of wool-bearing sheep by their plundering raids, but their first knowledge and practice of it were due to the later presence among them of the many Pueblos who had joined them in consequence of the restoration of Spanish rule in the last decade of the Seventeenth Century. The Pueblos, as we shall presently see, had long been familiar with the art, but up to that time the Navajos had known nothing of spinning and weaving.

ANOTHER STEP

FIGURE 15—"At San Ildelfonzo * * he built the first church in New Mexico"

THE Spanish writers who dealt with early events in New Mexico transmitted to us many misleading statements; but among their more accurate narratives, and the more interesting in connection with the present subject, are those relating to the introduction of sheep and of the weaving of woolen cloth, in that region.

Alvar Nunez Cabeza de Vaca was the first European to enter New Mexico. He was the treasurer of the fleet of Narvaez who had been commissioned by the King of Spain to undertake an expedition of conquest to the mainland of Florida. Misfortune beset the undertaking, and a part of the company, which had landed and which included de Vaca, having lost communication with the vessels, built boats in which to leave Florida. These were scattered by a storm, and late in 1528 de Vaca and his boat-crew were cast ashore on the coast of Texas where all were soon made prisoners by Indians. After six years of captivity de Vaca and three of his men escaped, and set out to make their way overland to their countrymen in Mexico; Cortez having invaded that country in 1519. Their course was northwest, and they evidently proceeded as far in that direction as central New Mexico, whence they made their way southward and reached the City of Mexico in 1536.

In his "Relacion" of his travels, de Vaca tells of having found linen and woolen cloth in use by the natives, and at one place on his journey fine cotton shawls; all of native production.

Friar Marcos in his account of his expedition into the Pueblo country in 1538 mentions the natives as being dressed in cotton cloth; and says the men of Cibola wore long cotton gowns reaching to their feet. He further states that he encountered later great numbers of men and women wearing cotton clothing, and that the people told them that others, living farther north, were dressed in woolen cloth; and also that they described a little animal which furnish the material of which the woolen cloth was made, Another report came to him of the people of Totonteac who dressed in woolen clothing like that worn by the Spaniards.

Coronado's expedition of 1540 traversed the country that had been visited by Marcos, and also went further north, into the "land of gold" of which Marcos had said he had heard; and in the account of this undertaking the natives are described as being dressed in cotton clothing.

Reports of Espejo's expedition of 1582 tell of native people encountered in the vicinity of the present city of Albuquerque, New Mexico, who dressed in striped cotton cloth; and say that Espejo received from one of their chiefs a present of 4,000 bolls of cotton, of which product the people are represented as growing large quantities.

The chief purpose of Onate's expedition was to colonize the territory now known as New Mexico. At San Ildelfonzo, an Indian village about ten miles south of Espanola, he built the first church and soon after founded a convent at the same place. Upon the return of the Spaniards in 1692, the old village was destroyed, and the people then moved just across the Rio Grande and established the village at its present location. The church built in the new village later is reputed to be a copy of the older one, and is shown in Figure 15.

The Pueblo Indian villages, mentioned in the preceding chapter, may not all now occupy their original sites, and they were known under entirely different names. The Spaniards gave them new names when they first occupied that region, and they are known to us only by the Spanish names. A majority of the villages are, however, located just as found by the invaders, and many of the buildings are known of record to be more than 300 years old, and it is not improbable that some of them have been in existence for at least 500 years. The walls are entirely of adobe, and the buildings are roofed with pine and cedar timbers covered with the same material as that of the walls. Comparing the present good condition of these mud buildings with the now dilapidated stone structures of the Cliff Dwellers, we have further evidence of the great age of the latter. In Onate's time the people living in this village were engaged in growing cotton and weaving cotton cloth.

Other Spanish adventurers tell of trading with the Pueblo Indians for sufficient cotton and woolen cloth to replace the worn out clothing of their soldiers.

There is no doubt that cotton flourished in New Mexico at the time mentioned. Recent experiments in the Territory demonstrated that it can now be grown there, and probably with profit. The weaving of cotton cloth by the Pueblos certainly was practiced long before the Spanish invasion, and as they had had no communication with any Europeans prior to that time, their art, unless inherited, must have had an independent origin and development among them.

The fact that cotton cloth of good weave and texture had been found among the older relics of the cliff people, throws the practice of the weaving art among races in, or that have been in, our southwest, far back into a very remote period. Accepting as possible, or even probable, the proposition that the Cliff Dwellers were the far-removed ancestors of the Pueblos, it would seem that the latter had inherited their knowledge of weaving, and had been weavers from an unknown time in the past. An especially fine specimen of

the Cliff Dwellers' weaving may be seen in the American Museum
of Natural History in New York.   This very interesting pre-historic textile fabric is a cotton blanket, that was originally about
three by five feet in size.   It was woven in colors, and has designs
similar to those on pottery found in the cliff dwellings; the designs
bearing some resemblance to those now used by the Navajos, but
which they derived from the Pueblos.   In color and general appearance this ancient cotton blanket also presents some resemblance
to Navajo work, but nothing very definite.

I have some specimens of the Cliff Dwellers' weaving that have
no designs and are without colors, made of a mixture of cotton
and yucca fibre.   Cotton and yucca yarn and rope have also been
found along with the articles above mentioned, buried in the sand
in burial trenches, and in the buildings, sometimes deep down under
the debris now forming the floors.

In my collection of Cliff Dwellers' sandals, which includes both
the plaited and woven forms, six different methods of making them
are to be seen.   Most of them are rough plaiting—in many instances
the different forms of basket weaving being illustrated.   A few,
however, show evidence of great skill.   The one illustrated in
Figure 5 is a rare and interesting member of the collection, one of
the pair of engraving showing the top, the other the bottom of the
sandal.   In this sandal appear designs in colors which are almost
in form with those found in some old Pueblo weaves and also similar
to figures in later work of the Navajos.   The designs show plainly
on the upper side of the sandal.   The lower side is remarkable in
the fact of having delicate raised zig-zag lines in the perfect pattern
of the Navajo lightning emblem.   The weaving is very skillfully
done, and would be a credit to an artisan of the present.   The warp
is threads of yucca—the woof evidently cotton, or some plant fibre
much finer and softer than the yucca.

That the early Spanish adventurers found, as they said, no
raw wool in the Pueblo country, is no doubt true.   No wool-bearing

sheep existed in North America until introduced by the Europeans; Cortez having brought the first sheep soon after the conquest of Mexico. The earliest Spanish colonists in New Mexico had taken cattle, horses, sheep and swine with them from Old Mexico and, as the climate was mild and the pasturage fair, the sheep increased rapidly and became a great source of wealth.

The Pueblos appear to have soon discarded the spinning of cotton for the easier spinning of wool, making many coarse woolen fabrics without any color, excepting the natural black and white of the wool and such shades as they could produce by a mixture of the two. At this time the Navajos had not become spinners and weavers. They made no fabrics of any kind excepting a rough plaiting of the leaves and fibre of the yucca and other plants. As they became possessed of sheep and learned spinning and weaving from Pueblos who had joined them, as already related, the Pueblos who had remained in their old homes turned their attention to the making of pottery as an art, and to herding cattle and tilling the soil as means of subsistence. Therefore the art of weaving declined among the Pueblos and, in the same ratio, was taken up by the Navajos. But some of the Pueblo women are still weavers, and the diagonal weaves of the Hopis are superior to any work done by the Navajos so far as texture is concerned.

The Hopi Pueblos use but few colors; and such blankets as they weave are of serape size, and ornamented with stripes only, the colors being blue, white and black, with sometimes a little red. The yarn is coarsely spun and the weaving loosely done. Many blankets that are shown as of Zuni or Hopi weave are made by the Navajos, being woven to conform to the fancy of the Pueblos. The Hopi women make a good black diagonal cloth used by them for dresses, and which is often beautifully embroidered in patterns that might have come from Persia. They also weave and embroider the kilts and sashes worn in the ceremony of the snake dance, and which are made of white yarn and embroidered in black, red and green.

With the exception of the two families, the Zuni and Hopi, none of the Pueblos now do any weaving worth mentioning. Probably, if the Pueblo Indians were shepherds, and were obliged to seek the most profitable disposition of their wool, they would compete with the Navajos in blanket-weaving. But as they lack the raw material, and are not much inclined to industry, it is quite likely that when the Navajo squaw folds her loom, which she will do before many years shall have passed, blanket-weaving among the Indians of our country will be at an end.

It is true that no form of primitive loom such as the Navajos now use is found among the Pueblo Indians, excepting with the Hopis and Zunis. When conditions influenced the other Pueblo tribes to stop spinning and weaving, the distaff and loom soon disappeared, for the indolent Pueblo Indian would not care to preserve anything he did not need, especially if it would make firewood. That all of them were weavers from an early period, there is no room for doubt, for the stories of the Spanish pioneers in that country agree in testifying that these people were found well supplied with woven cotton fabrics.

But the tales about woolen cloth being in use by the Pueblos at that time were evidently due to lack of care in ascertaining and recording facts. It is, however, possible that the llama or some similar animal capable of affording material for a fabric resembling one of wool, flourished in New Mexico in early times, and that it was cloth made of such material that the Spaniards supposed to be made of wool. But as there is neither knowledge nor tradition of the natives ever having had such animals, it is more probable that the woolly hair of the buffalo which was then common in that country, or the fur of the rabbit which may have been the "little animal" mentioned by Marcos, was used to make such cloth.

The hair of animals, and the feathers of birds, were woven

into the meshes of cotton fabrics found in the cliff ruins, but no threads of wool. Therefore it would seem that if the Pueblo Indians spun the hair or fur of animals, at all, it was an industry handed down by the pre-historic people.

It is interesting to note from the various relics found, and from accounts by the Spaniards, that some of the early native people of our southwest did not depend upon the skins of wild animals for clothing, but were spinners and weavers of such material at hand as could be worked into textile forms, no matter how rough or crude.

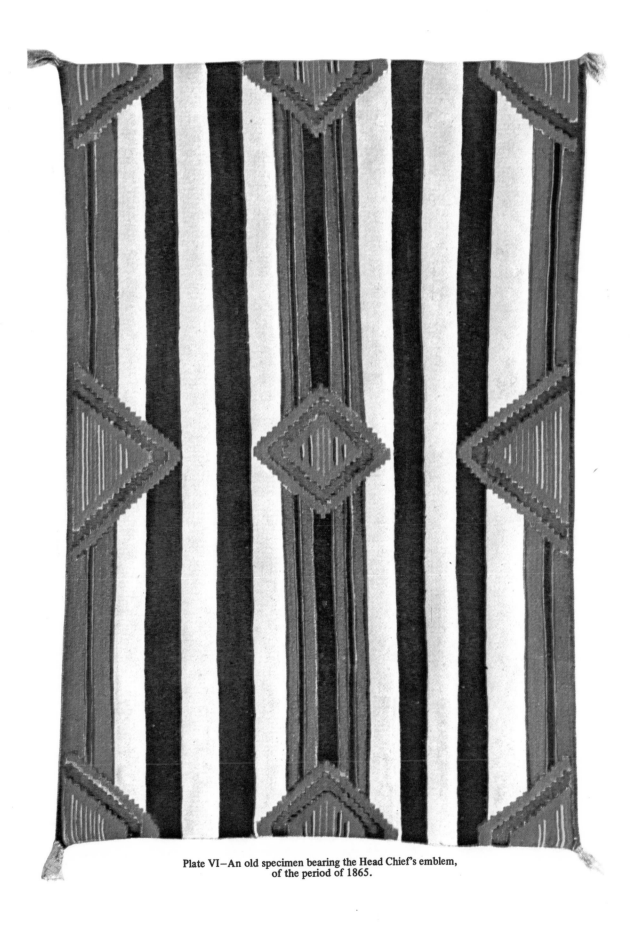

Plate VI—An old specimen bearing the Head Chief's emblem,
of the period of 1865.

THE BLANKET

FIGURE 16 — * * "there was then, as now, a Navajo flock in every valley"

THE Pueblo weaving was, as we have seen, the foundation on which the Navajos have built up an industry which has, as a barbaric art, assumed a position of considerable commercial importance. In spite of this fact, which has brought them into rather close contact with white men in disposing of their products, the native characteristics of these people other than their warlike traits have been less affected by association with civilization than the large majority of North American Indians; and to this we may ascribe the barbaric beauty of their woven patterns and the harmony of bright colors worked into them. As soon as they are influenced by the white man's taste to the extent of changing their patterns and colors, the beauty of the Navajo blanket will be doomed. Let us hope that it will be a long time before such influences become apparent in Navajo weaving.

It is frequently said that many of the so-called Navajo blankets are now made in eastern factories, but this is not true to any great extent. Some garish things in attempts at Navajo designs are so made, but the likeness is too poor to be called even an imitation; and no dealer with the slightest sense of honor would offer one of the horrid things as a Navajo blanket. Tourists have only themselves to blame if they are sometimes thus deceived.

The Navajos often prefer to wear blankets made in the east, for two reasons: one is that they are lighter; and the other, that they can sell a good blanket of their own make for a sum sufficient to purchase a "Mackinaw." Not long ago a lady visitor saw one of these Mackinaw blankets on the back of a Navajo buck at Gallup, N. M. She immediately began negotiations, and finally got the blanket for about three times what is cost "poor Lo," and went away rejoicing, believing she had a genuine Navajo blanket. Why? because she had bought it from a Navajo Indian! Incidents of this kind having been repeated frequently have, no doubt, given rise to the story and belief that a large proportion of what are said to be Navajo blankets are not made by the Navajos, but are the products of eastern looms. Nothing, however, can be further from the truth. A visit to the establishments of all the Indian traders in or about the Navajo nation, or to those in any of the cities of the east or west in which Navajo blankets are offered for sale, will fail to find a single blanket represented as of Navajo origin that was not made by the Navajos themselves.

The following letter from a prominent manufacturer of woolen blankets explains the situation to date, and seems to settle beyond question that no good imitation will soon be made:

"PENDLETON WOOLEN MILLS.

"Fleece Wool Blankets, Indian Robes and Shawls.

"PENDLETON, OREGON, June 23, 1902.

"DEAR SIR—We have your letter of the 17th and also the sample of the Navajo. We note what you say about blanket people saying this has never been successfully imitated. It is for a good reason. It is impossible with any machine yet made to get this effect. On our looms there are but two shuttle boxes on a side. Running a different shuttle in each box only allows for four colors at a time. In this robe a certain color appears and then is cut out. On a machine when a color once starts across the beam, it must be carried clear to the other side, either on one side or the other. If you lose it from the top, it must appear somewhere on the bottom. It is necessary for it to go clear across to be able to return. In weaving by hand, one can simply take the shuttle out any place desired and lay it aside until wanted again, covering the end between the filling threads and the warp.

"We can get this diamond pattern, however, if you think it would do, but cannot get the effect nor the weave as it appears in this robe. The Racine people are making a shawl something after this pattern, but can only use a limited number of colors, for the reasons explained above.

"We could do this. We could get something like this pattern and then work with two colors for a certain width, and then change to two others, giving a striped effect. For instance, we could work with black and yellow, the diamond or pattern appearing in yellow and the background in black, and then change to green and red, for a certain width, and so on. This, however, would not produce the effect you are after.

"On this kind of a proposition we can quickly tell you we cannot do anything except go ahead and try to get up something that is impossible. If you think a robe something like I have described would sell, let me know and we can get out some, but they will be far, far from the Navajo effect.

"Yours very truly,

"PENDLETON WOOLEN MILLS."

I have traveled extensively throughout our southwestern country, and have examined the stocks of nearly every Indian trader and dealer in Navajo fabrics; and in no instance has a spurious blanket or rug been offered me as of Navajo make. I have not always agreed with the dealers' statements regarding the age, composition or coloring of their blankets, but I am, however, pretty welly satisfied that in the main they are sincere in their representations, and place their goods before their customers with the best knowledge they possess. Some of them have been so long in the business that they are authorities upon the subject.

To know very much about the Navajo blanket in general requires about the same kind of experience that a diamond dealer goes through before he is able to tell a genuine stone at a glance. Indeed, the knowledge comes only through such experience, and is usually attended by more or less expense; though it gives much pleasure, even if you do have to pay for it.

To see your collection of blankets grow, knowing that each addition was made with a little better taste or skill than the preceding one, is a genuine delight.

The term "blanket" is used to describe everything of Navajo weave, chiefly for the reason that in the beginning, and for many years thereafter, the Navajo fabrics were made only in such sizes as could be used for a serape, or as a covering while sleeping. As the demand for them increased, smaller, or rug sizes, were made; and now, so far as relates to these two kinds, the latter are produced in much greater numbers, and are used almost entirely for the purposes of rugs. It would seem proper, therefore, to call the smaller sizes "rugs"; but as the term "blanket" appears to be fastened upon them by common consent, it is probably better and perhaps more convenient to use "blanket" as a general term for all the Navajo products, rather than to classify them under distinctive names.

The earliest reference to Navajo blankets, so far as I have been able to learn, written by any of our own people, is in Burdett's "Life of Kit Carson." In dealing with some events of the year 1840, he says:

"Carson now organized a party of seven, and proceeded to a trading post called Brown's Hole, where he joined a company of traders to go to the Navajoe Indians. He found this tribe more assimilated to the white man than any Indians he had yet seen, having many fine horses and large flocks of sheep and cattle. They also possessed the art of weaving, and their blankets were in great demand through Mexico, bringing high prices, on account of their great beauty, being woven in flowers with much taste. They were evidently a remnant of the Aztec race."

In his "Notes of a Military Reconnoissance," Major Emory, referring to his visit to Santo Domingo, New Mexico, in September, 1846, says:

"We were shown into his reverence's parlor, tapestried with curtains stamped with the likenesses of the Presidents of the United States up to this time. The cushions were of spotless damask and the couch covered with a white Navajo blanket worked in richly colored flowers."

It is likely that the "flowers" referred to by these writers had been embroidered on a white Navajo blanket by Mexican women.

In November, 1846, Emory encountered some Indians whom he thought were "Pimos Apaches," but as they were in a district then included in the Navajo country, and were engaged in spinning and weaving, probably they were Navajos. Of their methods of spinning and of their loom he says:

"A woman was seated on the ground under the shade of a cottonwood. Her left leg was tucked under her and her foot turned sole upward; between her big toe and the next, was a spindle about eighteen inches long, with a single fly of four or six inches. Ever and anon she gave it a twist in a dexterous manner, and at its end was drawn a coarse cotton thread. This was their spinning jenny. Led on by this primitive display, I asked for their loom by pointing to the thread and then to the blanket girded about the woman's loins. A fellow stretched in the dust, sunning himself, rose leisurely and untied a bundle which I had supposed to be a bow and arrow. This little package, with four stakes in the ground, was the loom. He stretched his cloth and commenced the process of weaving."

It is almost certain that Emory was mistaken in saying that the material being spun was cotton. As we have no record that the Navajos ever grew cotton, it is more than probable that these people were using wool, for there was then, as now, a Navajo flock in every valley. But this does not detract from the interest attached to this early observation of Navajo spinning and weaving.

Few, if any, who read this little volume will care to engage in weaving blankets as the Navajo women make them. But if one desires to engage in the work, an educational sojourn among the Navajos is necessary, and therefore I shall make no attempt to describe the process in detail, such as would enable a beginner to set up in the business. Many months of patient study and practice would be required before the first and simplest step, that of spinning, could be mastered; and then would come the coloring, and the slow, tedious work of weaving. I refer now only to the blankets made from the wool of the native sheep, which is sheared, spun, colored and woven by the Navajo women. Simple as it may seem at first consideration, the process as a whole is really intricate and puzzling; and if we measure successful results, only, we can hardly realize how much toil, physical suffering, and patient, painstaking work is involved in producing the thousands of these blankets that are being made annually.

The sheep are not washed before shearing, as is the practice with white people, and so there is no sheep-washing holiday among the Navajos. In late years they have used the white man's sheep-shears, obtained from the traders, to remove the fleece; but before these were procured, they pulled the wool from the sheep, or, by using a dull knife, party cut and partly pulled the wool away. The fleece is first tossed and shaken to remove the sand, then thrown over a rope or bush, and the burrs and other foreign material carefully picked out. The next process is washing, which is thoroughly done, the wool coming out clean and white.

At this juncture it may be said that that abnormal and much maligned creature, the "black sheep," is common in Navajo flocks and is looked upon with favor. Its wool is usually of a rusty black, but from some it is of a glossy, jet black; and this is highly valued on account of the saving of the labor of dyeing, and for its positive and enduring color.

When the wool is thoroughly washed it is spread upon mountain sage or greasewood shrubs to dry, and the next process is to prepare it for the cards. For a long time the Navajos have been able to procure from the traders the old-fashioned wire-toothed cards, such as were used by our grandmothers before the invention of the carding machine, and by which the wool was carded into rolls for spinning. A small handful of wool is made into an oblong form and then placed between the cards and rolled back and forth until a long, loose roll of wool is the result.

The manner of using the cards is shown in Figure 17, which is from one of Professor George H. Pepper's photographs, procured for the American Museum of Natural History by the Hyde exploring expedition.

The Navajos have no spinning wheels, though they are abundantly able to purchase them; and therefore their spinning is a slow process. For this part of their work they refuse all innovations, preferring to adhere to the methods that have come down to them through 200 years. Spinning the yarn is done with a simple distaff, which is a slender rod, about thirty inches in length and five-eighths of an inch in diameter, tapered to a spindle point at each end. It is usually made of a branch of the pinon, a dwarfish tree growing in the southern part of the Rocky Mountain region, the wood of which, when well seasoned, is as hard as oak and takes a smooth finish. A circular piece of wood, one inch in thickness and four inches in diameter, with a hole in the center, is slipped upon

the rod and fastened about twenty inches from the spindle end
proper. This is all there is to the Navajo spinning appliance with
which so much is accomplished; but by long practice they become
very skillful in twirling it and drawing out the thread at the same
time. When the thread is drawn out a sufficient length, the motion
is reversed and the thread wound upon the spindle, just as our
grandmothers used to reverse the wheel for the same purpose.
The manner of spinning, and the results of the first process, are
shown in Figure 18, which is also from a photograph procured
by the Hyde expedition for the American Museum of Natural
History.

The yarn produced by the first spinning is too coarse and too
loosely twisted to be of any use in weaving, and therefore it is
unwound from the spindle and spun again, and will then answer
for the coarse woolly weave we sometimes see. But a third spinning must be done before the yarn is in anything like fit condition
to work into a fine blanket; and for extra fine blankets, or for warp,
a fourth, and sometimes a fifth, spinning is required. From this
the reader may form some idea of the amount of work that must be
done by the Navajo slave of the blanket. When the yarn is finally
spun it is washed again, as the Navajos understand as well as the
whites that it will take color and work better if entirely free from
dirt and from the natural grease of the wool.

In getting ready for the work of weaving, the first step, after
preparing the yarn, is to construct the warp frame. This is made
a little larger than the blanket to be woven, and is of slender sticks
lashed together at the corners. It is laid upon the ground, and
the warp is wound upon it from top to bottom, the threads crossing
in the center; and it is then ready to set in the frame. For this
two posts are planted upright in the ground, and cross-beams are
lashed to them near the top and the bottom. At the top a mov-
abel pole is held horizontally to the upper frame timber by a rope
arranged spirally, so that by tightening or loosening the rope, the

FIGURE 17—A NAVAJO WOMAN CARDING WOOL

pole can be readily raised or lowered. The upper bar of the warp frame is fastened to this pole by loops of rope, and all is arranged so that in starting weaving the upper end of the warp frame is about twelve inches below the top of the main frame. The lower end of the warp frame is now fastened to the lower bar of the main frame, the warp being thus drawn taut. The loom proper is now complete, the warp is in place, and everything is ready for the beginning of weaving.

A stick wound with yarn takes the place of what our weavers call a heald. Twine is wound around it, taking in every alternate thread of warp, and when the heald is drawn forward it brings one-half of the warp threads with it, thus opening the warp for the more ready placing of the woof. They use no shuttle; the yarns of different colors being wound in balls, and these are passed back and forth between the warp threads in the same manner as the ordinary shuttle, excepting that they cannot be thrown, but must be slowly worked along by hand. If the reader will suspend a blanket of moderately intricate pattern, with the warp running up and down, and count across it the different colors and shades, and the repetitions of each, the number of the many little balls of yarn that were hanging on the face of the blanket while it was being woven will be known. The Navajo woman carries a color along until the pattern demands a change, when the first ball is dropped, after having made a loop of the yarn to prevent its unwinding, and the next color is taken up. This thread is drawn around the thread of the first color to preserve continuity, and thus the process goes on, back and forth, a single thread at a time passed in and out through the warp, the woof being laid loosely to prevent the weave from drawing in at the sides. As the work progresses, the yarn is beaten down in the warp by using a thin, hard stick as a batten, and the firmness of the weaving depends largely upon the use of the batten; the hard, almost waterproof, specimens indicating the conscientious application of this implement. This manner of weaving results in a single-ply fabric; the pattern being the same on both sides. Figure 19 is a picture of a Navajo weaver at her work, and was made from a photograph by Charles Goodman, of Bluff, Utah.

Sometimes the main frame of the loom is dispensed with, and the trunks of a pair of standing small trees are utilized in its stead. But this is of most primitive form, and lacks many of the features of an approved Navajo loom, though it serves to illustrate the simplicity of construction that may be made to answer the purpose.

While weaving, the squaw sits on the ground and weaves from the bottom upward. When the work has progressed so far that she cannot reach it easily, the rope on the upper beam is loosened, as is also the top bar of the warp frame, permitting the latter to slide down on the frame sides to the proper position. It is now fastened again, the warp drawn taut and the finished portion of the blanket sewn tightly to the lower beam of the main frame.

The reader may have often noticed the marks of this sewing, for it is done so tightly, and the blanket is held so firmly in position while being woven, that they remain for years, and frequently until the blanket is worn out.

Weaving is carried on wherever the family happens to be, and in caring for their sheep they are on the move a great deal of the time, seldom remaining more than four or five days in a place. When they are moving there is often seen on a single horse, a mother with two or three children, a pack of wool and yarn, and a complete loom. This scene is shown in the beautiful engraving used as the frontispiece to this volume, and made from a photograph by Mr. Matteson, which he has named "Homeward Bound."

When they stop the first thing to be done is to clear away a place for the loom and set it up. Sometimes in moving the woman will forget the idea of pattern she had had in mind for an unfinished blanket, and the result is an irregular weave. In other instances she may lose some of her yarns on the journey, and therefore must finish the blanket as best she can with the colors she has left. Such circumstances account for the irregularities we find in some really good blankets, especially among the older ones.

In considering the colors used I shall first refer to the period when many of the dyes were made by the Navajos themselves. Their first idea of high color came from the introduction of bayeta, a material, of which so much is and has been said and that is not now obtainable in the original form. It was entirely different from the so-called "squaw-cloth," samples of which are often shown as bayeta. Squaw-cloth is a coarse woolen stuff in many colors, and an attempt to ravel it and preserve the yarn in anything like a condition in which to be retwisted or respun, will demonstrate the fallacy of calling it bayeta, and of asserting that that material was ever used in making Navajo blankets. The genuine bayeta was entirely of wool, dyed with cochineal, and presented the various shades of red natural to that dye.

Cochineal, it is true, is a product of Mexico, but it must be remembered that the Spaniards had been in Mexico more than one hundred years before the Navajos ever possessed sheep, and even if Mexico was the only country producing cochineal there was plenty of opportunity to have introduced it into Europe. As it is, however, also produced in Java and in Algiers, the question sometimes raised, that, as cochineal was a product of Mexico, the bayeta brought from England could not have been dyed with it, is set at rest.

Cochineal produces both a brilliant scarlet and a crimson, according to the manner of treatment. A fact of interest in connection with this color is that a fabric dyed with it may be changed to an orange red by acids, and to violet by alkalis. This accounts for some peculiar colors in old weaves which can be accounted for in no other way.

The warp and woof strands of the old bayeta were of equal size, and so well spun that when raveled they were strong enough for weaving. In the old blankets of fine texture we find evidence that in many instances the threads have been respun to reduce their size, and in the case of heavier weave, the threads have been doubled and twisted. This readily explains the lack of uniformity we find in the weight of genuine old bayetas.

Bayeta was originally taken from Manchester, England, to Spain. From there it was sent to traders in New Spain, or Mexico, and by them bartered or sold to the Indian traders who had access to the Navajo country, where it was at first used only sparingly. It was expensive, and the labor required to ravel it, and the great care and skill required to handle it properly, led the Navajos to make only narrow stripes of bayeta in blankets of their earlier weaving.

Let us not confound the true bayeta with the modern squawcloth. The latter is now used by the squaws for dress skirts and by the bucks for leggings, and head-dresses and much beadwork made nowadays have the same cloth for a basis.

I have heard people talk about blue, green and yellow bayeta. but I have never seen a sample; neither have I been offered a blanket as bayeta in which these colors appear to the exclusion of the red. It is, however, a rule when showing a blanket in which the stripes or figures are of bayeta, to call it a bayeta blanket; the fabric taking its name from this precious bit of woof, no matter how small. The other colors may be good or bad; but that makes no difference. The blanket is a bayeta, as generally accepted. The reader may be quite sure, however, that if a blanket was made in the bayeta period, the painstaking skill required to treat the material was reflected in the spinning, coloring and weaving of the fabric; and if worthy to be called bayeta, it is apt to be a pretty good blanket all through.

The accompanying colored plates are reproductions, in design and color, of Navajo blankets in my collection, which at the present time numbers about seventy-five examples that have been carefully selected during the last twenty years.

Plate I shows one-half of a Navajo "squaw-dress," which belongs to the period between 1840 and 1860. It is a perfect specimen of bayeta and natural black wool, but the only symbols are those of mountains, in two forms. In size it is thirty-one by forty-one inches.

Plate II represents a very old example of Navajo work in "pink bayeta," native wool and native dyes. Its symbols are those of mountains, as indicated by the steps in the squares, and of lightning, the latter appearing in almost perfect designs. Color and form assign to this blanket a date about the year 1850. Its size is twenty-eight by forty-six inches. Of pink bayeta, which enters into the composition of this blanket, some account is given on a succeeding page.

It appears that in the primitive period of Navajo weaving only white wool was used in making blankets. In some later time the idea of stripes was suggested, and the wool from the black sheep was used to make narrow bands across the blanket. The next change was a mixture of white and black wool, making what we call "sheep's gray," which is found in very old blankets; and for many years thereafter only white, black, and gray appeared in the productions of Navajo looms.

It is quite safe to say that nearly all, if not all, Navajo blankets made prior to the year 1800 were without any colors, proper; that only undyed wool was used. The introduction of bayeta about that time, worked a change in the whole blanket scheme of the Navajos. They began to experiment with plants and roots; and colors, proper, were found. Following the weave by periods, as evidenced by age and texture, we find that yellow was the first of their native dyes. A light yellow was produced by steeping the leaves of the peach, and a brighter and more attractive one was made later from the flower heads of the Bigelovia Graveolens, a plant with great trusses of bright yellow flowers, and that grows profusely in the Navajo country. A darker yellow is now made from the root of a plant called by the New Mexicans "rabbit wood"; but I have not been able to find the plant, and do not know what it is.

When the early traders learned that the Navajos were seeking colors, they introduced indigo, and probably the dye-stuff known as Brazil wood. The latter was originally a red dye-stuff brought from the far east at a very early period. Later it was found by the Spanish General Cabral in South America, in the year 1500. The eastern product was called Brasil, Bresil and Brasile, names probably derived from the broken form in which it was first introduced. The wood was found in South America by the Spaniards, in the territory now known as Brazil, and this South American state was named by them on that account.

Its natural color is the mahognay red, seen in some very old blankets, and which has been attributed to native dyes. By mixing it with iron a purple is produced, and a good black is made by combining it with acids. With these additions to their list, fancy for designs was stimulated and the idea of symbols began to develop, but up to about 1820 there had been little attempt at symbolism in blanket patterns.

Having the blue and yellow, the Navajos learned to produce a green by combining the two, but there is no evidence that they ever made either a satisfactory blue or green of vegetable dyes alone. Indigo was to be had soon after they began to seek for colors; but green was rarely used in old weaves. A dull mahogany red found in many old blankets may be traced to the introduction of Brazil wood. As black became more popular on account of its

Plate VII—A valuable old bayeta blanket,
made about 1840.

symbolic importance they required more and of a deeper shade than was produced by the wool of their black sheep. This they were able to provide by a dye made by combining a decoction of the leaves of the sumac with a native yellow ochre and the gum of the pinon. In the very old weaves we find white, black, gray, blue, yellow and green only.

In collections of old blankets we occasionally find some of the bayeta period with stripes of rose or pink, which, for want of a better name, are called "pink bayetas." The term is correct only so far as it describes a blanket, the woof or warp of which has been raveled from other fabrics. While such blankets were not made from the cochineal-dyed bayeta, it is likely that the same material was used as in weaving bayeta, and that the weaving was very similar; but the dye was entirely different from cochineal. Close examination reveals the fact that at one time the color was a bright red, and that by long exposure to the sun and wind it faded or toned down to a rose or a pink hue. These blankets are rare, and are all in what we call "old Navajo" patterns or designs; and were made earlier than 1850. The one shown in Plate II is a good example of a pink bayeta fabric.

The predominating features in the pattern of Plate III are termed by some good judges the "Aztec Club" design; the barred lines being supposed to represent the war-clubs found in old so-called Aztec tombs. Another interpretation is that they mean a number of lodges, connected by ties of blood relationship; the central figures in white and black symbolizing an union of two families, with lineage running back many generations to two entirely different tribes.

This blanket is a curio. In age it antedates the use of commercial dyes by the Navajos. The single strand yarn of which it is entirely composed shows it to be of Navajo spinning.

The white and black, the natural colors of the wool; the yellow, no doubt produced by a decoction of peach leaves and bark; the pink, some combination of vegetable dyes, not common.

The size of this specimen is thirty-six by fifty-four inches.

It must be remembered that bayeta was expensive, and that it was due to this fact that so many very old blankets, that have this shade of red in their composition, have been preserved. In proportion to the number of antiques, the percentage of bayetas is large. They had cost more to produce, and were therefore valued more highly and better cared for.

There was no good red among the native dyes. If there had been, bayeta would never have been known as an element in a Navajo blanket. A reddish brown was made from the bark and roots of trees and shrubs, but no good red. Bayeta was undoubtedly the stimulus that led them on to other colors, and is without question the one thing more than all others that laid the foundation for the most beautiful aboriginal fabrics of our country.

We have now dealt only with the colors used in old blankets. These consisted of the imported bayeta, indigo, and Brazil wood, and the black, yellow, and green native dyes produced by the Navajos. This was in the substantial period, when coloring, spinning and weaving were more conscientiously done. The introduction of cheap, commercial dyes is an innovation to be deplored, as much in the Navajo land as in Persia. Like the beautiful fabrics of the Orient, our own barbaric weaves have suffered by the introduction of these inferior mineral dyes. We are glad to believe, however, that the worst period in this respect has passed, as there is a tendency on the part of traders to induce the Navajos to return to the old-time methods, and also to insist that when mineral dyes are used they shall be only of the best qualities.

Many of the innovation color effects from cheap commercial dyes are pleasing, but most of them are untrustworthy, and should have no place in a Navajo blanket. The reds are the most un-

FIGURE 18—A NAVAJO WOMAN SPINNING WOOL

reliable; and the purple, maroon, dove color, and bright orange, which are out of place among the colors that make a Navajo blanket a thing of beauty, are also the most disfiguring. If one is in doubt as to the stability of a color, the water test will settle the question. High prices are paid, as a general rule, for Navajo blankets, and buyers are entitled to the assurance of permanent colors. But the reforming influence must come from the purchaser, and when he insists, the trader will soon see to it that the Navajos use only fast colors. It is in the interest of all, the buyer, the dealer, the Indian trader, and the weavers themselves, that this be brought about as soon as possible.

The art of weaving is so old that history can tell us nothing of its origin. It was known by the inhabitants of New Mexico centuries before the coming of the Spaniards, and no doubt had been practiced by the Pueblo Indians long before the advent of the Navajos, who knew nothing of it until many years after they had taken possession of their present country. Their first knowledge of textile work followed the introduction of sheep, but not until after the Pueblo's insurrection, as we have no evidence whatever that they ever made thread or yarn of cotton or knew anything about it. Soon after that time the deserters from the Pueblos had become well established among the Navajos. These people had taken with them all the knowledge they possessed of spinning and weaving, but the Navajos were slow to adopt the work, and appear to have made but little progress in the first quarter of the Eighteenth Century. So far as can now be ascertained, they had not become able to produce a rough weaving sufficient for protection from the inclemency of the winter, until about the year 1720.

Then there was no sentiment, no symbolical figures, no color, nor beauty either in design or weave. The coarse fabric was made only to meet the demand for covering for their bodies. The Navajo squaw had not yet developed her artistic sense, and

it took many long years to accomplish this. But in the evolution
of the blanket from a coarse article of necessity to the beauty of
barbaric fancy, produced later, her whole nature was changed.
She had been slowly growing to be a slave of the blanket, but was
working out her destiny without knowing it. Gradually the spirit
of her work grew, with color and patterns springing into being—
colors and patterns that even astonished her; and she began to
weave her whole soul into the meshes of her work. Thus weaving came to be, with the Navajos, a woman's art entirely.

The severe plainness of the rough, early fabrics of white, or
of white and black—things of utility only and in the natural colors
of the wool—prompts us to ask what influence was at work in
the mind of the aboriginal woman that led her up from the level of
mere utility to the higher plane of color and pattern. It may be
that the Indian's love of high color inspired the first departure,
and that later on it was stimulated by a natural artistic instinct.
But she has been, to a certain degree, an imitator.

In many instances the designs on modern and ancient Pueblo
pottery have a semblance of color, but the colors are only sufficient to show what might be done in blanket colors. Possibly this
suggestion helped, and step by step the idea grew and took form,
and after a century of loving labor the superlative aboriginal product—the Navajo blanket—was born of a parentage of utility and
savage love of things beautiful. The poor woman of the mountains and plains must weave a blanket to sell, for she must live.
This does not detract from her artistic sense, nor prevent her
weaving the sad story of her life into the meshes of her work.
No one can read that record, and it is probable that she tells it to
no one. She lets it go out into the world, hoping, at least, it will
fall into the hands of some one who will care for it tenderly, even
though they do not know.

The principal designs are emblematic. However, the weavers do not feel closely bound to these conventions, but follow their

own fancies and conceits to the extent that each fabric holds an individuality.

The Navajo squaw is not a highly sensitive being. She is not romantic and not keenly alive to a sense of beauty, as is manifested by her lack of pride in her personal appearance, and the untidy condition of her house. Forlorn, unkempt, a willing drudge for her family, surrounded with nothing to stimulate a fancy for things beautiful, with not even the incentive of adequate reward to encourage her, there is, in spite of her environment, manifest in her work a subtle sense of color value, a correct estimate of proper color combinations, and an artistic conception of design that is wonderful. Barbaric it is, and properly so; even to the limit of gaudiness; but never lacking in perfect harmony of color.

The Navajo squaw is a child of nature. She follows no pattern. All the figures are evolved as she works, and as she weaves the story of her life. In symbolical figures she shows the mountains near which she was born; the river from which the water was taken in which her own and her Indian lover's hands were washed in the ceremony of marriage; the trees, clouds, rain, wind, whirlwind, and the lightning. She portrays the tortuous path man must travel to attain superiority. She knows the symbols that must appear in some form to adorn the blanket of a chief, the robe of a bride, or the mantle of the dead. The colors, stripes, squares and crosses and zig-zag diamonds are not meaningless designs. It is to be particularly noted that curves and circles are tabooed. Every design may be reduced to straight lines. The cross in some form is a common figure.

This is finely illustrated in Plate IV, which represents a curious as well as a rare old blanket. This fabric is composed entirely of bayeta, native wool colored with native dyes, and the sheep-gray mixture of white and black wool. The narrow stripes of dark red indicate use of either Brazil wood, or of a native dye the formula of which is now lost. The letter H appearing so prominently is only incidental to forming the numerous simple crosses of red. This blanket is undoubtedly of sacred significance, combining the creative elements of fire and water. It was woven about 1845, and in size is fifty by seventy-two inches.

The "swastika" or ansated cross, an evolution from the "Greek cross," so long the emblem of the Aryan people, appears on some very old Navajo blankets. But in thus directing attention to it I do not wish to be understood as implying that because the swastika is found on old Navajo blankets its presence is direct evidence that the Navajo is remotely of Asiatic origin. As the swastika appears on pottery found in the cliff ruins, it is possible that the Pueblos inherited it and transferred it to the Navajos. Therefore he who solves the problem of the origin of the Cliff Dwellers may also be able to account for the adoption and use of the swastika by the Navajos.

The true cross—with all arms of equal length—was found on vases and cotton fabrics of the Pueblo Indians when the Catholic Spaniards first visited New Mexico. Whether or not there be any relation between this and the torture cross does not affect the fact that the native people of our Southwest paid, and still pay, homage to the former as a symbol of protection, and also when directly supplicating the Great Spirit. Each of these forms is found on both the old and the new blankets, but the presence of the torture cross may, of course, be readily accounted for by referring it to the religious influences introduced by the Spaniards. A cross made of very narrow lines in a blanket is usually interpreted as indicating that an enemy had recently crossed the trail of the weaver's family.

Each of the various other figures and patterns woven into the Navajo blankets has its special significance. The diamond figure that appears in many pieces of their work distinguishes a page on which their tribal history is written. The wave pattern, easier described as following the lines of an old-fashioned rail fence, is one of the old symbols, and indicates the importance of water to animal and plant life. Squares remind us of the four quarters of the globe, the four seasons, and the "four winds," as they call the four points of the compass, from which they say the winds blow. These are also indicated by tassels at the corners of the blankets. The creative spirit in which is combined father and mother is shown in the colors red and black: fire, the father, in red; water, the creative mother, in black; and each also refers to the creation of the world as well as to the origin of plant and animal life. Black is also shown as the color of the north; and blue as the color of the south. Again, red is the male color, and blue the female color. A straight line with shorter bars dropping from each end, denotes the storm clouds; and the same figure inverted under it, is a mist rising to meet it. Zig-zag lines mean lightning, and a multiplication of these lines by intersecting them is known as the "rattlesnake" pattern, the snake among the Indians of the southwest being closely related to some form of worship. Lines forming steps mean mountains, and rows of little squares refer to Indian villages. The Aztec club pattern was once popular, being, as previously remarked, an effort to figure the Aztec war-club found in some of the old ruins. A border of complicated lines, often seen, is the rough road the Indian novitiate must travel before he is competent to sit with the warriors in medicine lodge or around the council fire. Obtuse angles, though rarely found, mean the sky.

Many of the Navajo blanket symbols evidently originated with Pueblo Indians, as we find similar figures on pottery made by them before the advent of the Navajo blanket. This was due to the influence of the Pueblo Indian recruits; although these figures were not produced in blankets until long after the Navajos began weaving. The figures are not exact copies from Pueblo pottery, but carry out the general ideas. Moreover, the emblems are

not placed according to rule, but are varied in position and arrangement to the extent that no two blankets are exactly alike; a
fact that supports the statement that the Navajo squaw does not
work from patterns.   That she does not is evident from the supplementing fact that in working she never has before her another
blanket from which to copy.

Pueblo Indian pottery shows many designs that the Navajos
do not reproduce.   Principal among these are circles and scrolls
by which the Pueblos indicate the wind and the whirlwind.   The
fret is one of their oldest designs.   The rectilinear fret, while
found on many blankets, is also found on basketry older than the
blanket age; but made by people far removed from the Navajos.
According to the best information we can get, fret designs indicate mesas and canons.   Inverted pyramids are the whirlwinds
as they descend into the canons.   Squares connected by lines indicate a number of families joined by ties of blood relationship.

The Navajo blanket is a gem of barbaric weaving.   Of a
startling combination of bright colors, it would be hideous except
for the perfect harmony in the arrangement of the colors.   There
may be faults of weave, texture, or pattern, but never really a fault
in the blending of colors.   Blue, or black, and white are effectively
used with colors in maintaining this harmony.

Plate V is from a modern blanket that has had ten years of
constant use on the floor as a rug.   It was made in 1891 of native
wool entirely, the colors being indigo blue, native black and analine red.   Its emblems are limited to those of mountains and
crosses, and its size is thirty-six by sixty inches.   This blanket
has been used on the porch a portion of the time, exposed to the
sun and wind, but has not changed color, except to soften a trifle.
It has been washed a number of times in the ordinary way of washing flannels, and, as may be noted, the red held its own, and did
not run into the white, as would have been the case if a very good

mineral dye had not been used. This is evidence that if the traders would insist upon the Navajos using only the best quality of mineral dyes there would not be much to be feared from them.

Plate VI is from a fine old specimen bearing the Navajo Head Chief's emblem, of the period of 1865, made of native wool; the colors being those of indigo and native dyes. These are the true old colors—black, blue, red and white. The design is the Navajo Head Chief's insignia of that period—intended only for the Chiefs, and, until recently, held sacred to their use.

The Navajo blanket is barbaric in effects, and that is chiefly why we like it. In perfect accord with itself, it seems to fit in almost any place. The only exception is that it would not be in good taste to use it in elaborately furnished rooms having delicate shades of finishings. The coarser grades make good rugs for the porch, and they can also be used to good advantage for lap robes, camp bedding, in country clubs and country homes, and on yachts. The finer qualities are desirable for portieres, especially for the door leading to the Indian or oriental room, or den. Some are fit to hang on the walls as pictures—as examples of the artistic conceptions that have been developed in the minds of untutored native women. As a rug on the stair landing, or on the floor of the hall or bedroom, as a covering for the couch or hall seat, or thrown over the stair railing, it seems at home; and in none of these places will it quarrel with its surroundings.

Some blankets seventy-five years old, and that have been in constant use, seem almost as good as new. The colors tone down with age like those of an oriental rug, and appear more beautiful because of age. This is one reason why connoisseurs are searching for old blankets; and another is that the weaves and colors of the old blankets are not reproduced in the new. Unfortunately, it was a custom at one time among the Navajos (but long since discontinued), to burn the belongings of the dead in the funeral ceremonies, and later to bury them with the dead; and in this manner many choice old blankets were destroyed. A large proportion of the really good old weaves that survive are now in the hands of collectors or dealers. A few may still be found among the Navajos, but most of these are old heirlooms that cannot be purchased at any reasonable price.

For more than a hundred years the Navajos have been disposing of their blankets in trade with the Mexicans and with the Pueblo, Ute and Apache Indians. Any one disposed to step beyond the traders and dealers in blankets to obtain rare specimens should not visit the Navajo country, but should go to the rural homes of the New Mexicans, to the community houses of the Pueblos, and to the tepees of the Utes and Apaches in almost inaccessible places in the valleys, the canons, and in the mountains, where travel must be afoot or on horseback. It is in these places that the finest old specimens now to be had from hands other than those of the traders, dealers, and collectors may be bought at prices not unreasonable in view of the rather eager demand at present prevailing for them.

With the exceptions noted above, the blankets to be obtained now directly from the Navajos are of modern weave. Indeed, most of them would be of very recent make—perhaps not more than two years old. But I do not mean to imply by this that the only desirable blanket is the old one, or that the modern blanket of good color is at all inferior to the old for ornament or use. The old blankets are sought for by connoisseurs and other people making collections, who are willing to pay well for humoring their fancies. The old blankets are not cheap, but new ones are, if the amount of skill and labor required to produce them be duly considered. New blankets of to-day will be old blankets by and by, and if carefully selected as to weave, patterns and colors, will grow in value each year. My interest in Navajo work was awakened twenty years ago, and at that time I sought only such pieces as pleased my senses of colors and figures, and, as a rule,

FIGURE 19—A NAVAJO WEAVER

selected new ones, because the colors were brighter and the patterns more complicated. It was several years before I realized the truth that old and sometimes tattered specimens were in certain respects more desirable and really worth more than the new ones, in the light of fancy as well as in intrinsic value.

However, I have some blankets in my collection that were not old when purchased, between fifteen and twenty years ago, but which were prudently selected, that show signs of toning down in color; and as the roughness is worn off, they now vie in appearance with the older ones, and would bring in the open market many times their original cost.

Plate VII shows a valuable old specimen in excellent state of preservation, with colors of indigo blue, bayeta and the dull mahogany red of Brazil wood. It was made about the year 1840 and is forty-five by sixty-eight inches in dimensions.

The beautiful blanket represented by Plate VIII is a fine example of the combination of bayeta, native wool and "Germantown" yarn.. The red is bayeta; the white and black, native wool; and the green and yellow, Germantown. This was made about 1870, near the close of the bayeta period and in the beginning of the use of commercial yarns among the Navajos. The emblems signify mountain ranges enclosing many lodges protected by water and by the "Lightning Spirit." The blanket measures forty-nine by sixty-one inches.

Good Navajo blankets, and inferior ones also, will be found in the stocks of dealers in Indian "curios" anywhere in the West. But it should be remembered that no genuine Navajo blanket is altogether bad. All are more or less characteristic, but some are coarse and loosely woven; and these are cheap in proportion to their coarseness. But nearly all late native-wool blankets appear coarse as compared with the old bayeta or modern Germantown fabrics. If the yarn be well spun and the weave close and firm, the native-wool blankets will, if used as rugs, tone down in color, wear smooth with use, and increase in value for many years. As opportunity occurs for careful examination of the stocks carried by dealers, one may gradually learn the distinctive features of modern Navajo weaving. But if one becomes interested in studying the products of different periods, visits should be made to private collections to understand well the whole scheme of color, design or weave.

Mr. B. G. Wilson, of Albuquerque, N. M., has a collection of quite wide range and which includes many rare specimens. But the finest exhibit within my knowledge, one covering from the earliest period down to the present time, and probably the finest collection in the world, is that of Seligman Brothers, of Santa Fe, N. M. My own collection of about seventy-five pieces has been carefully made and includes nearly the whole extent of Navajo weaving; a good representation of the development of the art through a period of seventy-five years.

The Navajo weaves may be divided into four general classes: The very old in natural colors, the bayeta, the native wool with native dyes, and the Germantown. By "native wool" is meant wool taken from the Navajo sheep; by "natural colors," the natural black, white and gray of the wool; the term "bayeta" is applied to blankets in which more or less of this material is shown without regard to the area of other colors; by "native dyes" is meant the colors made by the Navajos without outside assistance, and as indigo has always been used with the colors produced by them, it is included among the native dyes to avoid confusion; and by "Germantown," blankets woven of the commercial "Germantown" yarn."

The old blankets may be, for convenience, divided into the early and the later types with respect to their patterns, though the reader will remember that the first ones made were plain white fabrics. The early-pattern blankets have broad stripes of black and white only—the crude, first conception of design. The sec-

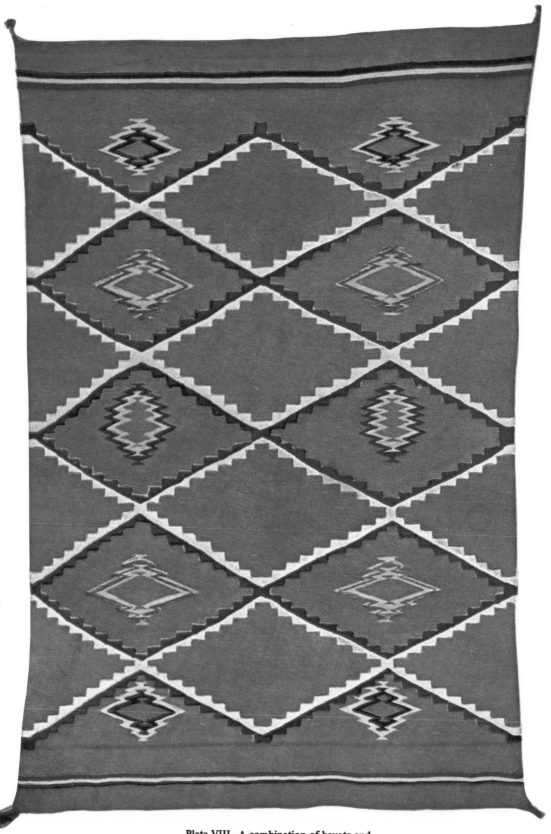

Plate VIII—A combination of bayeta and
Germantown yarn.

Plate IX—A Navajo beauty, wholly of Germantown yarn;
about twenty-five years old.

ond, or later, type consists of broad stripes of white, black, and gray; the latter having been made by mixing the two natural colors of the wool, and thus marking the second step toward pattern-design.

The bayeta blankets may also be separated into two divisions. The first, or older, has narrow stripes of the bayeta red alternated with wider stripes of the natural colors; stripes constituting the entire pattern effect. In the second, or later, we have the beginning and the development of complicated designs in which the conception of symbols made its first appearance; and from this beginning has grown the somewhat elaborate system of symbolical figures that is now established as characteristic of Navajo blanket designs. The bayeta went into its decline about 1860, but did not pass entirely out of use until 1875.

The native-wool and native-dye blankets originated and developed in the same period as that of the bayetas, but outlived them. The native-dye period continued undisturbed until the introduction of commercial dyes, about 1875, and since then there has been no distinct class period. For some native-wool blankets the native dyes were exclusively used; for many others both the native and the commercial dyes were used; and for still others the commercial dyes provided all the colors employed. There are, also, some blankets made of a combination of native wool and of the ready-dyed Germantown yarns. The native-wool and native-dye blankets are good, both in texture and color, for when the Navajos went through the trouble of making the dyes they valued the yarn sufficiently to prompt them to great care in spinning and weaving it, which accounts for the finer texture of the older weaves. But when they later learned that they could color yarn with but little trouble by using mineral dyes, they became somewhat careless, both in spinning and weaving, and the result in many instances was a blanket below the standard acceptable to lovers of barbaric art.

The fourth, or Germantown, class is one not to be ignored. When introduced the fabric was called the "innovation blanket." It is made of so-called Germantown yarn entirely, in all of the fanciful colors sent out by the mills, and if the colors be well selected, keeping as closely as possible within the lines recognized as those of Navajo colors, these blankets are worth more than passing attention. Their bright colors and superior weave commend them to all who care for decorative Navajo blankets. They were first made about the year 1875, but only a few had been produced prior to 1880. I have one of the older of this class and it has held its colors remarkably well, toning down sufficiently to add much to its beauty.

This fine blanket, which measures forty-four by fifty-six inches, is brilliantly represented by Plate IX, and is now of great value on account of its age. It was used on the floor as a rug for six years, and has hung on the wall the remainder of the time, but is now handsomer than when purchased. As a general rule, blankets of this class are fringed at both ends, the fringe being made of the same yarn and colors as appear in the blanket. The service of this blanket has proved the excellence of its weaving and of its Germantown ready-dyed yarns, and also that it is not a mistake to buy a thoroughly good piece of Navajo weaving of Germantown yarns when a beautiful pattern in brilliant colors is desired in combination with great durability.

In Plate X is shown another fine example of Navajo weaving entirely of Germantown yarn. In this the pattern follows closely the lightning design, but the weaver has sacrificed the symbol for harmony of effect, so that in this detail the work is somewhat imperfect; but the mechanical evenness of the points and spurs shows great skill and care. The points on the sides indicate that in the weaver's family-clan were many lodges. She was long celebrated for her skill, but during the closing years of her life made only small specimens. This one is only twenty-seven inches square, and was made about 1890.

No blanket of Navajo weaving is fringed except the German-town. All others have little tufts or tassels at the corners, and it may often be noticed that old blankets, made half a century before Germantown yarn was introduced, have little tufts of that yarn on the corners. The old tassels having been worn away, the squaw replaced them immediately with such yarn as she had at hand. They are symbolical of the four corners of the world, and she cannot permit the symbols to be absent from a blanket with which she has anything to do.

In selecting blankets, if possession of the better grades only, be desired, one should guard against buying anything having a cotton warp. This was quite popular with the Navajos for a time, beginning about 1880, but the best Indian traders have discouraged the use of it, and the tendency now is to return to woolen warp, in weaving both native-wool and Germantown blankets. Many good-looking blankets yet in the market have this stain upon their lineage, but it can be detected by opening the woof sufficient to expose the warp. It is often the case, however, that wool warp is spun so hard that at first gla nce it may be mistaken for cotton, and a close examination is needed to determine which is which. Blankets have been offered me as old ones, showing the marks of wear and of age, that might have deceived me only for the tell-tale cotton warp that places them in a later period.

It should not be assumed that because a blanket is worn full of holes and has a pattern of uncertain red, that it must, of neces-city, be an old bayeta. Many comparatively new ones have seen such hard usage that they are in a sadly dilapidated condition. As a general rule the Navajos are not particular to take good care of an ordinary blanket retained for their own needs, but use it as a saddle blanket, or for protecting grain exposed to the elements, or as a covering for the earthen floors of their hogans. On the contrary, and as a rule, the finer ones have been carefully cared for, and, in many instances, laid away and kept for generations without being devoted to any use. This accounts for the perfect conditon in which we find many old specimens. I have one almost solid bayeta that can be traced back to 1848, and which has the appearance of having just come from the loom. We rejoice to find a pedigreed blanket. That is, one that we can trace in ownership back to the time it was made, and the more distant the period, the more satisfactory is the blanket. There are many such, well authenticated, that can be traced as far back as 1825. I take great pride in one of mine that was brought home by a soldier who had served with Kit Carson in the troublous times of 1863, and kept by his family until two years ago.

The sizes of Navajo blankets vary from twenty-four by thirty-six inches—the common saddle blanket size, to fifty-four by eighty-four inches—for serapes. Intermediate sizes are made for use as rugs, and are so made only because the white man wants to buy them in such sizes. But some very large fabrics are woven, as large as eight by ten feet, in most instances to order, for covering a porch or a hall. They are usually thick, coarse and heavy, and will give good service. An interesting fact connected with these great fabrics is that it is safe to assume that no two are exactly alike. Therefore the possessor of a good and pleasing one has the satisfaction of being quite sure that no one else in the world has one just like it.

Occasionally when a dealer has found a typical old pattern that he wishes to continue in the market, he sends it out into the Navajo country to have a number made like it. In a measure he succeeds in getting about what he wants, but as the weavers are not accustomed to working from patterns, they make some mistakes. Therefore while the copies as a whole are rather uniform in general appearance, a close comparison always proves that no two are precisely alike. However, this is such a departure from the general usage, and the dealer so soon tires of seeing a number of blankets around his place so nearly similar, that the experiment is seldom repeated.

The Navajo "squaw-dress" is of especial interest. It is made in two pieces, each of which is usually about thirty by forty inches in size. They are sewed together on one side, the other being left open, and the "dress" worn wrapped around the body, with the open side on the right. The upper right-hand corners are fastened together over the right shoulder, which holds the opposite, or closed side, up under the left arm. The center is black, generally the natural black of the wool, but the ends are always woven in red. The typical squaw-dress has only the two colors, red and black, the reds at the ends of the two fabrics being ornamented with symbolical figures to suit the fancy of the weaver. As they do not make many of these now, the majority offered for sale are old ones, the ends of which are very apt to be bayeta. There are, however, a few recent ones to be had, which can be distinguished by the coarser yarn used in the red, and the general appearance of newness.

The Arizona branch of the Navajos have been sending out within a recent period a well-made and attractive blanket that has been represented to be of woven goat-hair, or of a mixture of goat-hair and wool. I do not know who is responsible for the deception. Possibly it was the dealer who first introduced and sold carpet yarn to the Indians; for that is what it is. But the blanket should not be condemned on account of the deception, for it is a good one, promising fast colors and great durability; and may be classed in order of merit with the Germantown.

Woven into certain old and almost priceless Navajo fabrics we find three colors, red, yellow and green. Judging from the peculiarity of texture, and of the shades of colors used, which are unlike anything else we find in Navajo work, these weaves and their colors antedate the bayeta and the yellow and green of the native dyes. All the colors are strong, and quite unlike anything found in blankets of later weaving. They are traced to discarded army uniforms—the scarlet coat of the infantry, the yellow of the cavalry, and the green of the medical staff. In all countries there are times when army clothing is sold for anything it will bring, and in cases where the colors are such as to be attractive to primitive people it is purchased by traders for barter. It is quite evident that some of this second-hand clothing was utilized by the Navajos in the same manner as the bayeta was treated by them later—raveled and worked into blankets. The supply available to them apparently was quickly exhausted, and it appears to have been soon followed by the bayeta period and the production of native vegetable dyes. These blankets are probably the oldest in existence in which high colors appear, and are exceedingly rare. In all my research I have seen only two, but have learned of the whereabouts of several others. One of the two that I have seen is valued at $1,000.

We must consider any blanket woven by the Navajos as a Navajo blanket. To be sure there would seem to be a more correct sentiment associated with one the material of which was sheared from a Navajo sheep, the wool carded, spun and colored, and the fabric woven by a Navajo squaw, than there is in a blanket woven of Germantown or of carpet yarn, by the same squaw. But this is only a matter of sentiment, and leaves each of us free to be governed by our different fancies in making selections; and if each pleases himself, the others should rest content.

CONCLUSION

FIGURE 20—* * "the young Navajo woman in her bridal array"

THE general purpose of this little volume has been fulfilled in the preceding pages so far as I had in view when it was undertaken; which was to give some account of the Navajo people, of their myths, legends, and traditions, of their country, their manners and customs, and especially of their exceedingly interesting principal industry.

Beyond presenting the substance of their folk-lore concerning their origin, history, and so forth, I have not attempted to deal with it as a subject, nor do I intend doing so in these concluding pages. But I ask the reader's indulgence while I refer briefly to some curious and perhaps suggestive elements in their stories of the past, and in certain of their present beliefs, customs and practices, the outlines of which have already been related.

While it is evident that these have been but little affected by what we may call American civilization, it is impossible to determine to what extent they have been influenced by the somewhat long-existing associations the Navajos have had with the Pueblos and other tribes around them; and by the less intimate contact with Spaniards and Mexicans. The more potent of these influences probably would have come from that strange people, the Pueblos, of whom there are still a considerable number of decadent tribes or clans in our southwest country. We have seen that the Navajos derived their knowledge of spinning and weaving from them, and also that many circumstances suggest that it is not altogether improbable that the Pueblos may be far-removed descendants of remnants of the race of Cliff Dwellers, from whom they would have inherited primitive arts, beliefs and customs. Therefore any attempt to deal with Navajo folk-lore would bring the Pueblos into the discussion.

The intelligent visitor to the Pueblo country finds it difficult to avoid an impression that the objects and scenes before him have in them something, which he cannot define specifically, that reminds him of those of the Asiatic cradle-land of the human race. The intangible things which artists call "atmosphere," and "local color," are here the atmosphere and local color of western Asia; and the aspects of a group of pueblo buildings (Figure 21) amid dreary surroundings are strangely like those presented in pictures of life and places in that old land.

The ruined buildings and minor relics of the Cliff Dwellers offer much evidence in support of the theory that those people were of Asiatic origin; and among the Pueblos are found what seem to be links of a broken chain that once connected them with the older people; and some of which are also present among the Navajos.

In the weaving done by the Cliff Dwellers, in that by the Pueblos, and that by the Navajos, there is a similarity in certain respects, but in all there is a suggestion of Asiatic fabrics; though for the purpose of such a comparison the Pueblo and the Navajo weaving should be considered as one. Figures delineated on the Cliff Dwellers' pottery resemble those on ceramic objects made in Asia long ago, and which also appear on some of more recent production there. The rectilinear fret that is present in various modified forms on much of their pottery, is the same as that employed by the ancient Greeks in detail ornamentation of their architecture.

This fret-figure, as are others of the designs on the Cliff Dwellers' products, is common on Pueblo pottery and in Pueblo weaving; and from that source it is evident that the Navajos, who use it in their blankets, derived it. Moreover, the familiar Greek scrolls and spirals are duplicated in both Cliff Dweller and Pueblo ornamental work. The Swastika, often figured by the Cliff Dwellers on their pottetry, and also by the Pueblos on their pottery and in their weaving, and from the latter borrowed by the Navajos, is too strange an emblem to have had an independent origin among either the Cliff Dwellers or the Pueblos. To the latter, and also to the Navajos, it has practically the same significance it possesses for the Hindu.

Those of the Cliff Dwellers' dwelling-places that were chiseled out of the great bluffs of rock, are significantly like the Rock Temples of India which were formed in the same manner; and their built-up structures are not without similarity to old edifices that survive in Asia and northern Africa.

As were the Cliff Dwellers, the Pueblos are communal, but their clan-dwellings are not built in recesses in cliffs. They stand in the open, sometimes on top of a small mesa that resembles a truncated isolated hill having precipitous sides.

Turning now to consideration of the elements in the Navajos' folk-lore to which I have referred, we may perhaps find in them a drift or tendency toward implying an Asiatic origin for these people also. But I do not ask attention to them in the spirit of a partisan, nor do I place myself in the attitude of a special pleader for the proposition.

In the myths, legends, and traditions of all peoples there are absurd tales, contradictory variations, and more or less confusion, which render very uncertain any result of an attempt to reduce them to a consistent form representing probabilities; and, as the reader has seen, those of the Navajos with relation to their origin and to their migration to their present country are not free from such defects.

The belief that their progenitors came out of the earth, if intended to account for their "creation," is not inconsistent with our own lingering myth that man was made "of the dust of the ground," and implies for their theory the same Asiatic origin to which we are indebted for ours. The conception of the earth as the mother of all living things appears to be as old as mankind, but it is not clear that the Navajos have this in mind when they use an expression equivalent to "our mother land," as they are intruders in the country they now occupy.

The belief referred to in the foregoing was common to many of the Indian tribes of the western half of North America, though some of them interpreted it as meaning that their ancestors lived within the earth at first, but by their skill and cunning succeeded in making their way out to the surface.

The two Navajo traditions of their ancestors' migration to this continent, one that they came by water, and the other that they crossed a narrow sea beyond the setting sun and landed on the northern shores of this country, may be regarded as one and the same reminiscence. If the story be entitled to serious consideration it would, of course, suggest that the pioneer Athabascans, from whom the Navajos descended, crossed at Bering's Strait, or by way of the chain of Aleutian Islands. The fact that that family of Indians has so long occupied the western part of British America lends some support to this theory of their Asiatic origin.

The myth of the "ship-rock" or "rock-ship" provided by the Great Spirit, and upon which the Navajos were carried high in the air to their present country, yields to no reasonable conception of a source from which it could have arisen, nor of an event which could have served as a basis for it. However it is possible that the ship idea in the story may have been suggested by some vague knowledge of Asiatic legends of the deluge and Noah's ark.

FIGURE 21—A VIEW IN ZUÑI

The other tale, in which the Navajos' forefathers are represented as having been brought from the north on the back of a swift and obliging great bird, reminds us of some of the adventures of Sinbad as related in the "Arabian Nights" stories, and of fables which tell of small birds riding on the backs of large ones in certain emergencies in ornithological history; "as an eagle stirreth up her nest, fluttereth over her young, spreadeth abroad her wings, taketh them, beareth them on her wings."

That these intrepid aerial navigators were guided in their migration by a messenger from the sky is nothing new, for there are other legends of primitive peoples having been so favored in their wanderings. Moreover were not Moses and his unruly horde led in the way by heavenly pillars of smoke by day, and pillars of fire by night?

While the Navajos have been, within narrow limitations, influenced by contact with those who professed the Christian religion, their real religious beliefs are bound up in their worship of the heavenly bodies and the powers of Nature. Their adoration of these is consistent with the practices of nearly all primitive races, but in it are some features that would seem to be related to old-time faiths of western Asia and of the Mediterranean region, where Sabaism attained its greatest development and influence.

One of the conceptions of the Navajos is that of the sun as the Father and the earth as the Mother of all life; and this is exactly paralleled by an ancient Greek belief. Another, in which the moon takes the place of the earth as the Mother, is the same as that of oriental peoples of antiquity by whom the moon was regarded as the sun's wife.

The most important duties of the Navajo medicine man are those of a priest of the sun, and in this capacity he is the "Shaman." An ancient Hebrew name for the sun was "Shamesh" or "Shemesh." Whether this consanguinity of terms and their application is significant in connection with what we are considering here I shall leave to the reader for decision.

The requirement that the door of the permanent winter hogan must face to the east is plainly associated with sun-worship, but for this the Navajo home-builder has many illustrious examples among the ancient temple-builders of the Mediterranean region. The Hebrews of antiquity fronted their tabernacle, shrines, altars, and tents to the east, and the main portal of Solomon's barbarically decorated "house of the Lord" was illuminated by the light of the rising sun.

The Navajo altar with its motley appendages and curious embellishments, before which all religious ceremonies are conducted, may represent in some of its details the effects of modern religious influences, but to the Navajo mind it has a general significance and certain associations which would not have been derived from that source, but seem to be connected in a misty way with ancient oriental ideas.

The close relation of the snake with the Navajos' religious beliefs and forms of worship is another factor in the stock of arguments used by those who attribute a remote Asiatic origin to these people. It is true that the Navajos may have adopted the Pueblos' snake superstitions, just as we have taken over and made our own the old Hebrew version of the story of Eve's disastrous indiscretion, but they deny that they did so.

When the young Navajo woman in her bridal array (Figure 20) joins the young man—not of her choice, but who has made a satisfactory deal with her father for her—in the marriage ceremony of eating a cake or loaf, is there in this custom a reminiscence of the ancient Babylonians' offerings of bread or cakes to Ishtar, their goddess of the planet Venus—the goddess of sexual relations? Among the Babylonians these cakes or loaves were specially prepared for her, and were called "the bread of Ishtar."

The use of water in the Navajo marriage ceremony might be

referred to knowledge of the baptismal rite acquired from modern religious practices, were it not known that the custom antedates the Spanish invasion of that region. Sometimes the medicine man pours water on the hands of both the bride and groom; at other times the groom applies the water to the bride's hands; and at still others they lave their hands together. But "living water" from a spring or running stream must be used. The conceptions upon which all baptismal beliefs are founded are of extremely remote antiquity, and the rite can be traced ages back of the period with which Christian people usually associate its introduction. Possibly the Navajos may have borrowed this custom from the Pueblos, but they claim it as their own from immemorial time, and I have not been able to learn that the present-day Pueblos observe it.

The color symbolism of the Navajos would also seem to have some connection with oriental peoples, but as they derived their knowledge of spinning and weaving and also the principles of their designs from the Pueblos, it is probable that much, though not all, of their color-symbolism came from the same source. Undoubtedly the Navajos have developed and extended it, but the fact remains nevertheless that oriental astrological influences appear to be present in the associations connected with it. Red and black stand for the creative spirit in which is combined the father and mother elements; red for fire, the creative father; black for water, the creative mother. Each of these colors correspondingly refers, also, to the creation of the world as well as to the origin of plant and animal life. In other words there is here laid down the absolute true biological proposition that there must be heat and moisture in combination in the production of living things. Furthermore black is the color of the north, and blue of the south; while red is the male color, and blue the female. It is difficult to believe that such conceptions, that have their counterparts in oriental astrology, had an independent origin among the native people of our southwest country.

The reader may recall a juvenile belief that beneath each end of the rainbow "a pot of gold" might be found buried in the earth. The Navajo in a less worldly, a less selfish, spirit thinks that at each end of the bow messages from the Great Deity may be received. Did not Noah receive a promise-message from his God saying "the waters shall no more become a flood," and is not the rainbow "the token of the covenant?"

It is evident that the Navajos derived the foundations of their notions about their goddess "Assunnutli"—"the woman in the sea," from the Pueblos who, in turn, probably had them from more ancient people, or directly from the Aztecs. The name is plainly an Aztec word, and its association with the woman in the sea would be improbable from a Navajo standpoint, as these people have long lived far inland. Crediting her with having given blue corn to the Navajo men and white corn to their women is probably an idea of their own. The double sexuality attributed to Assunnutli has its parallel in more than one ancient Asiatic belief, and figured in the primitive Hebrew conceptions of Jehovah. The Aztec name for the sun was Nahuiatl, and it has been supposed that Assunnutli was a moon-goddess; the full moon's rising as seen from the coast of Mexico making it appear that the goddess was coming up out of the sea to greet her faithful worshipers.

The Navajo legend associated with their abstinence from fish as food would also seem to have an Aztec basis, upon which was erected the story about the bodies of enemies killed by pioneer Navajos having turned into fish. In the Aztec legend of the deluge we are told that "when the sun Nahuiatl came there had passed away four hundred years, plus two ages, plus seventy-six years. Then all mankind was lost and drowned, and found themselves changed into fish." However when the great freshet was at its height, Ishtar "wailed like a child," and cried, saying "I am the mother who gave birth to men, and, like the race of fishes, they are filling the sea!"

Plate X—Another fine example of Navajo weaving,
entirely of Germantown yarn.

The Navajos' veneration for birds, which is almost equivalent to a worship of them, and the belief that they serve as messengers to and from the deities, constitute a form of superstition that prevailed generally among our Indian tribes. Probably it grew out of the mysterious power of such creatures to rise and move rapidly in the air which, to the untutored mind, afforded no support to anything having weight, and offered no resistance to a falling body, as when one dropped from a tree or over a cliff, which had, no doubt, often been demonstrated in personal experiences. Seeing birds soar high above the earth would naturally lead primitive men to the conclusion that while up there so near to the abode of the gods they would certainly have opportunity to communicate with them, and would surely do so. Possibly Navajo regard for birds may be imperfectly connected with the same myth that has given the descendants of the dove which bore to Noah the "pluckt off" olive branch in her mouth, something like a sacred place in our esteem. Moreover it would not be polite in us to smile at the Navajos' bird-superstitions while we attribute to the piratical eagle virtues of which he never dreamt.

Concerning their regard for the bear as a sacred animal, I have nothing to add on my own account to what has been said in an earlier part of this volume—that it is probably due to unhappy consequences of attacking so formidable a beast with the ineffective weapons they possessed in early times. However it has been suggested to me that if our Navajo friends really are of Asiatic descent, the sacred character they attribute to bears may be in recognition of the service rendered by animals of that species in avenging the insult twice hurled at the prophet Elisha by the little children who came forth out of Bethel apparently for that purpose. But I disclaim any share of responsibility for this theory.

The Navajos' name for their tribe, "Tinnai" or "Tinneh," plainly connects them with the Indians of the northwestern parts of North America, and some people think they can detect in it an

Asiatic flavor. However that may be, the word is identified easily with the crude languages spoken by tribes in the northwest, including some in Alaska. Its definition, "the people," is the familiar one that was self-assumed by most of our other western Indians, also, as that of the tribal names they bore. Egotism and self-admiration persuaded each general family to believe and proclaim its people as "the people," in the sense of being the great people, greater than any other, the "chosen people" of an appreciative, and perhaps a partial, Great Spirit; and even sub-divisions of families asserted over their brethren a distinction based upon the same exalted theory. In holding to this complacent and perhaps inspiring belief our Indians were not alone among savage or barbarous races of men.

In various minor customs, beliefs, and practices of the Navajos, in which are included their ceremonies in dedicating a newly-built winter hogan, their refusal to dwell in habitations with which death is associated, their sepulture in tomb-like cists and in caves which is attended by a purpose to preserve the bodies, and their use of fetiches to increase the fecundity of their domestic animals—the latter, which is not a custom among most other tribes of Indians, reminding us of Jacob's employment of a fetich to bring forth "cattle ringstreaked, speckled, and spotted," at the expense of Laban's interest in the flocks—there might also seem to be some hazy reminiscences of ancient life in far-eastern lands.

The conservatism and intelligence of the Navajos may entitle their myths, legends, traditions, and so forth to more consideration than should be given those of inferior tribes, but even these do not serve as very satisfactory material with which to construct the framework of their history. As heretofore mentioned, their native characteristics, other than those which formerly made them warlike and persistent marauders, have not been greatly changed by their rather exclusive pastoral life. The influences of civilization that have crept to the borders of their reservation have not seriously disturbed nor spoiled them, and notwithstanding their

FIGURE 22—NAVAJOS GAZING UPON A RAILROAD TRAIN
(From the painting by F. P. Sauerwen)

present somewhat composite physical character in consequence of a limited amalgamation with neighboring tribes, they have as a people retained to a remarkable degree their old-time mental traits and habits of thought—they are still Navajos.

When they first heard of the white man's railroad train it was hard for them to obtain even a glimmer of comprehension of what it possibly could be. For several years after the roads penetrated the general region in which their reservation is situated, a popular Navajo diversion was to make pilgrimages in parties on horseback to gaze in wonder, from a presumably safe distance (Figure 22), upon the strange, dragon-like object which rushed along upon two narrow streaks of metal that marked a slender line across the country.

It is to be deeply regretted that so much of the history of the native races of our country is clouded in obscurity. Indeed, we know very little about it. Study of our Indian people was long neglected, and many opportunities to do so and that probably would have been fruitful, were irretrievably lost. The old Indian life which permitted the tribes to roam at will over vast areas is a thing of the past in the United States, and the changed conditions under which these people are now living are working among most of them corresponding great changes in their modes of life, manners, customs, beliefs, and in everything else that pertains to them.

It is only in the broad empire of arid territory in our southwest that we may now find the native tribes, though restrained within definite boundaries, living in much the same manner, observing much the same customs, and following much the same daily routine, that they did long before the reservation system had begun to hedge about and revolutionize Indian life and character.

It is also in that empire of arid wilderness that exist in profusion the ruined great memorials and countless lesser relics of a vanished people who were as strange, if we correctly interpret the testimony of what they left there, as any who have lived upon this earth; and around whose history and fate hangs a mystery as puzzling as any that ever shrouded a part of ancient humanity. The mystery associated with the Cliff people may forever remain unsolved, but the region in which they once lived, and the peculiar tribes which abide now in and around it, will long afford abundant material for fascinating research and study to all who are interested in the history of the human race.